100 CAROLS FOR CHOIRS

Edited and arranged by
David Willcocks and John Rutter

MUSIC DEPARTMENT

OXFORD
UNIVERSITY PRESS

INDEX OF TITLES AND FIRST LINES

Where first lines differ from titles the former are shown in italics.

Carols suitable for unaccompanied singing are marked thus ★.

OXFORD
UNIVERSITY PRESS

Great Clarendon Street, Oxford OX2 6DP
198 Madison Avenue, New York, NY 10016, USA
Oxford is a trade mark of Oxford University Press

Processed and printed by
Halstan & Co. Ltd., Amersham, Bucks., England

The following items may be considered for use at seasons other than Christmas:

Advent: A spotless Rose (p. 26), Adam lay ybounden (p. 32), Angelus ad virginem (p. 46), Lo! he comes with clouds descending (p. 206), Lo, how a Rose e'er blooming (p. 210), O come, O come, Emmanuel (p. 230), Out of your sleep (p. 263), The truth from above (p. 342), There is a flower (p. 333), There is no rose (p. 332).

New Year (secular): A New Year carol (p. 122), Deck the hall (p. 72), Here we come a-wassailing (p. 124), The twelve days of Christmas (p. 246), Wassail song (p. 362), What cheer? (p. 372).

Epiphany: As with gladness men of old (p. 52), Kings of Orient (p. 370), The shepherds' farewell (p. 344), The three kings (p. 346).

Passiontide: I wonder as I wander (p. 169), Sans Day carol (p. 219), The crown of roses (p. 376).

Easter: Jesus Christ is risen today (p. 197), Joys seven (p. 316), Lord of the Dance (p. 138), Sans Day carol (p. 219), This joyful Eastertide (p. 343), Ye choirs of new Jerusalem (p. 380).

Annunciation: Angelus ad virginem (p. 46), Ave plena gracia (p. 54), Gabriel's message (p. 315), Hail! Blessed Virgin Mary (p. 132), O Queen of heaven (p. 282), The cherry tree carol (p. 200), There is a flower (p. 333), There is no rose (p. 332).

The *Carols for Choirs Words Booklet* contains the texts of the following items, for use by congregation or audience:

A great and might wonder; A merry Christmas; All my heart this night rejoices; Angels from the realms of glory; As with gladness men of old; Away in a manger; Birthday carol; Child in a manger; Ding dong! merrily on high; Gabriel's message; God rest ye merry, gentlemen; Good King Wenceslas; Hark! the herald-angels sing; Here we come a-wassailing; I saw three ships (*both versions*); In dulci jubilo; In the bleak mid-winter; Infant holy, infant lowly; It came upon the midnight clear; Jesus Christ is risen today; Jingle, bells; Joy to the world!; Kings of Orient; Lo! he comes with clouds descending; Lord of the Dance; O come, all ye faithful; O come, O come, Emmanuel; O little one sweet; O little town of Bethlehem; Of the Father's heart begotten; Once in royal David's city; Personent hodie; See amid the winter's snow; Shepherds, in the fields abiding; Silent night; Sing aloud on this day!; Star carol; Sussex carol; The first Nowell; The holly and the ivy; The twelve days of Christmas; This joyful Eastertide; Unto us is born a Son; While shepherds watched their flocks; Ye choirs of new Jerusalem.

commissioned by the Cardiff Polyphonic Choir in association with the Welsh Arts Council

1. A babe is born
(Op. 55)

Words 15th century

WILLIAM MATHIAS
(b. 1934)

†or Piano duet, with 2nd player taking the pedal part only.

Also available separately (X222)

him   we sing both night and day.

Ve-ni Cre-a - tor Spi - ri-tus,

Ve-ni Cre-a - tor Spi - ri-tus,

Ve-ni Cre-a - tor Spi - ri - tus.

†Piano duet: Add lower octave in pedal part throughout.

3. There came three kings out ___ of the East, ___ To

wor-ship the King that ___ is so free, With gold and myrrh and

S. A

A. A so - lis or - tus car - di -

T. A so - lis or - tus car - di - ne, ___ car - di -

B. frank - in - cense, ___ A so - lis ___ or - -

babe is born all___ of a may,___   To

bring sal - va - tion___ un - to   us.   To

him we sing both night and day.

2. A child is born in Bethlehem
(Puer natus in Bethlehem)

Vv. 1 and 2 by DAVID WILLCOCKS
(V. 1 tr. from the Latin)
Vv. 3 and 4 from *The Cowley Carol Book*

SAMUEL SCHEIDT
(1587–1654)
edited by DAVID WILLCOCKS

If preferred the piece may be sung a tone higher.
Source: *Cantiones Sacrae Octo Vocum*, 1620

An SATB version (arr. Carter) is also available separately (X323).

*(orig. ♩ in all voices)

★orig. F (♮) not A

3. A great and mighty wonder

Words by ST GERMANUS (634–734)
tr. J. M. NEALE

14th-century German melody
harmonized by M. PRAETORIUS
(1571–1621)

full and ho-ly cure!
vir-gin-hon-our pure.
yet re-mains on high!
shep-herds from the sky.

Re-peat the hymn a-gain!

full and ho-ly cure!
shep-herds from the sky.

'To God on high be glo-ry, And peace on__ earth__ to men!'
earth to

3. While thus they sing your Monarch,
Those bright angelic bands,
Rejoice, ye vales and mountains,
Ye oceans clap your hands.
Repeat the hymn again! etc.

4. Since all he comes to ransom,
By all be he adored,
The Infant born in Bethl'em
The Saviour and the Lord.
Repeat the hymn again! etc.

5. And idol forms shall perish,
And error shall decay,
And Christ shall wield his sceptre,
Our Lord and God for ay.
Repeat the hymn again! etc.

See No. 50 (p. 210) for alternative text.

4. A maiden most gentle

Words by ANDREW CARTER★
(*b.* 1939)

French traditional melody
arranged by ANDREW CARTER

★paraphrased from The Venerable Bede

Also available separately (X266)

-ve Ma - ri - a, A - ve, a - ve, a - ve Ma - ri - a.

Voices unaccompanied

p

2. How bless'd is the birth of her hea - ven - ly__ child,__ Who came to re-

p

- deem us in Ma - ry so__ mild. A - ve, a - ve, a - ve Ma - ri -

- a,__ A - ve,__ a - ve,__ a - ve Ma - ri - a.

mf

Ped.

39

TENORS and BASSES

3. The arch - an - gel Ga - briel fore -

43

-told by his call The Lord of cre - a - tion, and

47

SOPRANOS and ALTOS

Sa - viour of all. A - ve, a - ve, a - ve Ma - ri -

Man.

52

-a, A - ve, a - ve, a - ve Ma - ri - a.

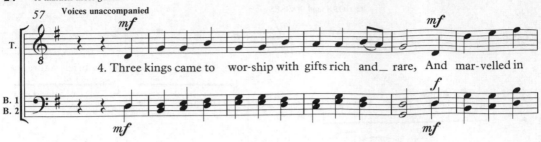

57 Voices unaccompanied

4. Three kings came to wor-ship with gifts rich and _ rare, And mar-velled in

63

awe at the babe in her __ care.

SOPRANOS

A - ve, a - ve, a - ve Ma - ri -

ALTOS 1 & 2

A - ve, a - ve Ma - ri -

69

- a, A - ve, a - ve, a - ve Ma - ri - a.

- a, __ A - ve, a - ve Ma - ri - a.

Ped.

75

ALL VOICES (unis.)

5. Re - joice and be glad at this Christ-mas we __

80

89(97)

*Composer's note 1997: The original (Choir 1) melody printed in earlier editions at this point, is best omitted altogether in favour of clean harmony and a strong soprano descant. The tune is in any case present for the most part in the tenor line.

to my mother

5. A spotless Rose

HERBERT HOWELLS
(1892–1983)

Words of 14th-century origin

might __ The

Maid; __ For | through our God's great __ | love __ and might The __
         | through   our God's great |

through our God's great __

dim. - e - **rit.** - -

Bless-ed Babe __ she __ bare __ us In a cold, __ cold __

Babe   she

S.

win - ter's night. __

A.

win - ter's __ night. __

T.

win - ter's night. __

B.

win - ter's night. __

Gloucester 22.10.1919

6. A virgin most pure

English traditional carol
arranged by CHARLES WOOD
(1866–1926)

SOPRANO
ALTO

TENOR
BASS

1. A__ vir - gin__ most pure, as the pro-phets do tell, Hath__
2. In__ Beth - le - hem__ Jew - ry a ci - ty there was, Where__

brought forth a__ ba - by, as it hath be - fell; To be our Re -
Jo - seph and__ Ma - ry to - ge - ther did pass, And there to be__

- deem - er from__ death,__ hell,__ and__ sin, Which A - dam's trans -
tax - ed with__ ma - ny one__ mo, For__ Cae - sar com -

- gres - sion had__ wrap - ped us__ in. *Aye, and there - fore__ be__*
- mand - ed the__ same should be__ so.

*In verse 4 the dotted slurs do not apply.

18

mer - ry; Re - joice, and be you mer - ry; Set__ sor - row__ a -

22

- side; Christ Je - sus__ our__ Sa - viour was__ born__ at this__ tide.

3. But when they had entered the city so fair,
   A number of people so mighty was there,
   That Joseph and Mary, whose substance was small,
   Could find in the inn there no lodging at all.
       Aye, and therefore, etc.

4. Then they were constrained in a stable to lie,
   Where horses and asses they used for to tie;
   Their lodging so simple they took it no scorn,
   But against the next morning our Saviour was born.
       Aye, and therefore, etc.

5. The King of all kings to this world being brought,
   Small store of fine linen to wrap him was sought;
   And when she had swaddled her young son so sweet,
   Within an ox-manger she laid him to sleep.
       Aye, and therefore, etc.

6. Then God sent an angel from heaven so high,
   To certain poor shepherds in fields where they lie,
   And bade them no longer in sorrow to stay,
   Because that our Saviour was born on this day.
       Aye, and therefore, etc.

7. Then presently after the shepherds did spy
   A number of angels that stood in the sky;
   They joyfully talkèd and sweetly did sing,
   'To God be all glory our heavenly King.'
       Aye, and therefore, etc.

7. Adam lay ybounden

PETER WARLOCK
(1894–1930)

Words 15th century

1. A-dam lay y-boun-den, Boun-den in a bond: Four thou-sand win-ter Thought he not too long. 2. And all was for an ap-ple, An ap-ple that he took, As

for the Birmingham Singers' Club

8. Alleluya, a new work is come on hand

Words 15th century

PETER WISHART
(1921–84)

No. 3 of *Three Carols* (OCS 899)

9. Angelus ad virginem
(Gabriel to Mary came)

Tr. W. A. C. PICKARD-CAMBRIDGE★

14th-century Irish carol
arranged by DAVID WILLCOCKS

★Slightly adapted

© Oxford University Press 1978

49(53)

mp SOPRANO SEMI-CHORUS

3. Ad haec vir - go no - bi - lis Re - spon - dens in - quit
3. Then to him the maid re - plied, With no - ble mien__ su -
'An - cil - la sum hu - mi - lis Om - ni - po - ten - tis
'Lo! the hum - ble hand - maid I Of God the Lord__ e -

p

Ah

p

52

1st time   *2nd time*

e - i: De - i. Ti - bi coe - le - sti nun - ti - o,
-per - nal, -ter - nal! With thee, bright mes - sen - ger__ of heav'n,

1st time   *2nd time*

Ah

Ah

Ah

59

Tan - ti se - cre - ti con - sci - o, Con - sen - ti - ens, Et
By whom this won-drous news__ is giv'n, I__ well a - gree And

Ah

Ah

10. All my heart this night rejoices

Words by PAUL GERHARDT (1607–76)
tr. CATHERINE WINKWORTH

JOHANN GEORG EBELING
(1637–76)

1. All my heart this night re - joi - ces
2. Hark! a voice from yon - der man - ger,
3. Come, then, let us has - ten yon - der!
4. Thee, dear Lord, with heed I'll che - rish,

As I hear, Far and near, Sweet - est an - gel voi - ces:
Soft and sweet, Doth en - treat, 'Flee from woe and dan - ger!
Here let all, Great and small, Kneel in awe and won - der!
Live to thee, And with thee, Dy - ing, shall not per - ish;

'Christ is born!' their choirs are sing - ing,
Breth - ren, come! from all doth grieve you,
Love him who with love is yearn - ing!
But shall dwell with thee for ev - er,

Till the air Ev - 'ry - where Now with joy is ring - ing.
You are freed; All you need I will sure - ly give you.'
Hail the star That from far Bright with hope is burn - ing!
Far on high, In the joy That can al - ter nev - er.

11. As with gladness men of old

Words by
W. CHATTERTON DIX
(1837–98)

Abridged from a chorale, *Treuer Heiland*,
by C. KOCHER (1786–1872)
arranged by DAVID WILLCOCKS

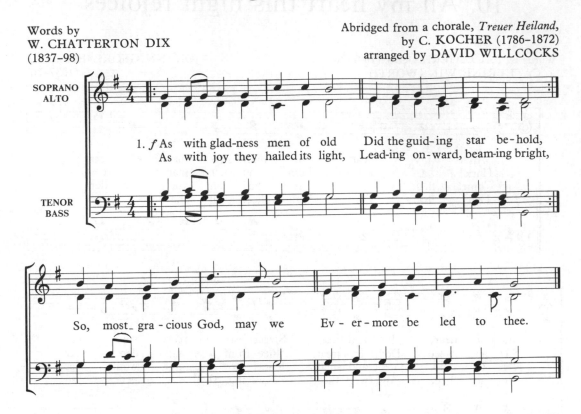

SOPRANO
ALTO

1. *f* As with glad-ness men of old   Did the guid-ing star be-hold,
As with joy they hailed its light,   Lead-ing on-ward, beam-ing bright,

TENOR
BASS

So, most gra-cious God, may we   Ev-er-more be led to thee.

2. *mf* As with joyful steps they sped
     To that lowly manger-bed,
     There to bend the knee before
     Him whom heaven and earth adore,
     So may we with willing feet
     Ever seek thy mercy-seat.

3. *mp* As they offered gifts most rare
     At that manger rude and bare,
cresc. So may we with holy joy,
     Pure, and free from sin's alloy,
     All our costliest treasures bring,
     Christ, to thee our heavenly King.

4. *p* Holy Jesu, every day
     Keep us in the narrow way;
cresc. And, when earthly things are past,
     Bring our ransomed souls at last
     Where they need no star to guide,
     Where no clouds thy glory hide.

The harmonies used for verses 1–4 are from *The English Hymnal*. It is suggested that verse 4 be sung by the choir only, unaccompanied.

Also available separately (*Six Christmas Hymns* arr. David Willcocks)

12. Ave plena gracia

Words 15th century

PETER MAXWELL DAVIES
(b. 1934)

Always quiet
Tempo I ♩ = 76

SOPRANOS (FULL)

★ORGAN (manuals) *Optional*

A - ve, a - ve ple - na gra - ci -

poco rit.

- a,___ A - ve, De - i ma - ter Ma - ri - a.___

Tempo II ♩ = 104

SOPRANO SOLO

1. Hail be thou, Ma - ry most of ho - nour, Thou ba - re Je - su our___

poco rit.   **Tempo II**

___ Sa - viour, Ma - ri - a.____ Hail be thou, mai - den, mo - ther and

poco rit.

wife,__ Hail be thou, stin - ter of our strife,__ Ma - ri - a.___

★The organ part, when used, should not merely "double" the voices, but add a bright silvery sparkle to them, the registration approximating as nearly as practicable that of an eighteenth-century chamber organ.

The music is published by arrangement with Messrs. Boosey & Hawkes Ltd.

Tempo I

continued overleaf

continued overleaf

13. Away in a manger

Words anon.
(19th cent. American)

Melody by W. J. KIRKPATRICK
(1838–1921)
arranged by DAVID WILLCOCKS

In verse 3 the whole choir may hum whilst a treble soloist sings the words.

14. Nativity carol

Words and music by
JOHN RUTTER

Also available separately (X169) and in arrangements for unison voices (U154) and SSA (W91)

star___ He___ who loved___ us so.___   Far_ a - way___
rare,___ Hearts with his warmth he fills.___

si - lent he lay,___   sempre cresc.

si - lent lay,___   Born_ to - day,_ your hom - age
si - lent he lay,___

si - lent lay,___   sempre cresc.

sempre cresc.

(omit small notes on piano)

15. Child in a manger

Words by
JOHN RUTTER

Celtic traditional carol
arranged by JOHN RUTTER

*Left-hand part may be played by any suitable instrument. If clarinet is used in v.1, bassoon could be used in v.2. (A fully scored version is also available on hire.)

Also available separately

7(17)

Sent from the high   - est,   Come down in glo - ry;
Of - fer your hom - age,   Kneel down be - fore   him;

9(19)

1st time

Tell the glad sto - ry,   Wel-come the   child.
Praise and a - dore   him,   Be not a -

12

2nd time

- fraid.

22 S. *mp*
A.
Ah _____ Ah
T. unis.
B. *mp*
3. Wise men, come seek him — Christ, our Re-deem - er;   Jour-ney to Beth - lem,

Led by a star.   Of - fer your trea - sures: Gold, myrrh, and in - cense,

Ah   *Ah*

Ah

Pre-cious ob - la - tions   Brought from a - far.

p   *cresc.* - - - - -

4. Praise to the Christ - child;   Praise to his mo - ther;

f

f

mf   *f*

Glo - ry to God our Fa - ther a - bove.
Fa - ther a - bove.
Fa - ther a - bove.

An - gels are sing - ing Songs of re - joi - - cing,

dim.

mf più dolce   **rall. al fine**   *p*   *dim.*

Greet-ing the in - - fant Born of God's love.

mf più dolce   **rall. al fine**   *dim.*   *p*

mf   *dim.*   *p*

16. Deck the hall

Welsh traditional carol
arranged by DAVID WILLCOCKS

1. Deck the hall with boughs of hol - ly,
2. See the flow - ing bowl be - fore us,
3. Fast a - way the old year pass - es,

Fa la la la la, fa la la la,

'Tis the sea - son to be jol - ly,
Strike the harp and join the cho - rus,
Hail the new, ye lads and las - ses,

Fa la la la la, fa la la la.

Fill the mead cup, drain the bar - rel,
Fol - low me in mer - ry mea - sure,
Laugh - ing, quaff - ing all to - ge - ther,

Fa la la la, fa la la la la,

Fill the mead cup, drain the bar - rel,
Fol - low me in mer - ry mea - sure,
Laugh - ing, quaff - ing all to - ge - ther,

Fa, fa la la la la,

Troll the an - cient Christ - mas ca - rol,
While I sing of beau - ty's trea - sure,
Heed - less of the wind and wea - ther,

Fa la la la la, fa

Fa la la, fa la la la la.

fa

fa la

17. Jingle, bells

Words and melody by
J. PIERPONT (1822–93)
arranged by DAVID WILLCOCKS

Also available separately (X315)

Jin-gle, bells, jin-gle, bells, jin-gle all the way; Oh, what fun it is to ride in a
Jin-gle, bells, jin-gle, bells, jin-gle all the way; Oh,____ what fun in a

jin-gle all the way; Oh, what fun in a

one - horse o - pen sleigh!____ Jin - gle, bells, jin - gle, bells,
one - horse o - pen sleigh!____ Jin - gle, bells, jin - gle, bells,

one - horse o - pen sleigh!____

jin - gle all the way; Oh, what fun it is to ride in a
jin - gle all the way; Oh,____ what fun it is to ride in a

way; Oh,

Repeat Verse 1 D.S. (p. 73)

one-horse o - pen sleigh!

Repeat Verse 1 D.S. (p. 73)

mf   *cresc.*   *f*

⊕CODA *(from p. 74)*

cresc.

Oh, what fun it is   to ride in a   one - horse   o - pen

_____ what fun it is   to ride in a

ff

cresc.

Oh,

⊕CODA *(from p. 74)*

cresc.   *ff*

allargando

sleigh! _____

allargando

Tpts.

sffz

18a. Ding dong! merrily on high

Words by
G. R. WOODWARD
(1848–1934)

16th-century French melody
arranged by DAVID WILLCOCKS

Also available separately (X196)

*i-o pronounced ee-o

Words reprinted from *The Cowley Carol Book* by permission

18b. Ding dong! merrily on high

Words by
G. R. WOODWARD
(1848–1934)

16th-century French melody
harmonized by CHARLES WOOD
(1866–1926)

1. Ding dong! mer – ri – ly on high in heav'n the bells are
   Ding dong! ve – ri – ly the sky is riv'n with an – gel

2. E'en so here be – low, be – low, let stee – ple bells be
   And i – o,* i – o, i – o, by priest and peo – ple

3. Pray you, du – ti – ful – ly prime your mat – in chime, ye
   May you beau – ti – ful – ly rime your eve – time song, ye

(1.) ring – ing:
     sing – ing.

(2.) swung – en,
     sung – en.

(3.) ring – ers;
     sing – ers.

Glo – – – – – – ri – a, Ho – san – na in ex – cel – sis!

*i-o pronounced ee-o

Reprinted from *The Cambridge Carol Book* by permission

19. God rest you merry, gentlemen

v. 1 Unison
v. 2 Harmony

English traditional carol
arranged by DAVID WILLCOCKS

1. God rest you mer - ry, gen-tle-men, Let no-thing you dis - may, For
2. From God our heav'n-ly Fa - ther A bless-ed an-gel came, And

Je -sus Christ our Sa - viour Was born up - on this day, To save us all from
un-to cer - tain shep - herds Brought ti - dings of the same, How that in Beth-le -

Sa-tan's power When we were gone a - stray:— O ti - dings of com - fort and
- hem was born The Son of God by name:— O ti - dings of com - fort and

com-fort and   *Verse 5 overleaf*

joy,— and— joy,— O— ti - dings of com - fort and joy.

Unison

3. The shepherds at those tidings
    Rejoicèd much in mind,
And left their flocks a-feeding
    In tempest, storm and wind,
And went to Bethlehem straightway
    This blessèd babe to find:
    O tidings of comfort and joy.

Harmony

4. But when to Bethlehem they came,
    Whereat this infant lay,
They found him in a manger,
    Where oxen feed on hay;
His mother Mary kneeling,
    Unto the Lord did pray:
    O tidings of comfort and joy.

★If preferred, the refrain may always be sung in unison (with organ accompaniment).   **Verse 5 overleaf**

Also available separately (*Five Christmas Carols* arr. David Willcocks)

SOPRANOS

Ah *Ah*

ALTOS

Ah *Ah*

TENORS
and
BASSES
(with
CONGRE-
GATION)

5. Now to the Lord sing prai - ses, All you with-in this place, And

ORGAN

Sw.

Gt.

Ped.

Ah *Ah* *Ah*

Ah *Ah* *Ah*

with true love and bro-ther-hood Each o - ther now em - brace; This ho - ly tide of

20. Shepherd's pipe carol

Words and music by
JOHN RUTTER

Available separately (X167)

Also available in the following arrangements:
1) S.S.A.A. voices (W76)
2) Unison voices with optional descant (U133)
3) Unison voices with easy accompaniment, shortened and simplified (U141)
4) Solo voice with slightly simplified accompaniment (Oxford Solo Songs)

3. 'None may hear my pipes on these hills so lone - ly

On the way to Beth - le - hem;___ But a King will hear me___

play sweet lul - la - bies When I get to Beth - le - hem.'___

91

Is it far to Beth - le - hem?'

mp

93 **G** An - gels in__ the sky__ brought this mes - sage nigh: 'Dance   and

An - gels___   brought this mes - sage: 'Dance   and

96 sing__   for joy   that Christ   the   in - fant King is

sing___   for joy___   that Christ   the   King   is

born this night in low - ly___ sta - ble yon - der,

Born for you at Beth - - - le - hem.'___

21. Wexford carol

Irish traditional carol
arranged by JOHN RUTTER

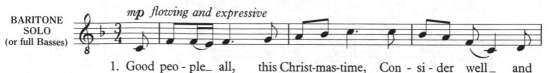

This setting may be sung a semitone higher.

Also available separately

BARITONE SOLO
(or CHOIR I TENORS)

Good peo - ple___ all,   this Christ - mas - time,   Con -

dim.   *pp*   Hum

(Hum)   dim.   *pp*

- si - der well___   and   bear in mind   What   our   good_ God   for

us   has done,   In   send - ing his___   be - lov - ed   Son.

rall.   dim.   *p*

22. Good King Wenceslas

Words by
J. M. NEALE
(1818–66)

Melody from *Piae Cantiones* (1582)
arranged by DAVID WILLCOCKS

Also available separately (X314)

**BASS SOLO or
FULL BASSES (and TENORS)**

mf

2. 'Hi - ther, page, and stand by me,   If thou know'st it, tell — ing,

mf

(Man.)

Yon - der pea - sant, who   is   he?   Where and what his dwell – ing?'

**SOPRANO SOLO or
FULL SOPRANOS (and ALTOS)**

mf

'Sire, he lives a good league hence,   Un - der-neath the moun – tain,

Right a-gainst the fo-rest fence,   By Saint Ag-nes' foun — — tain.'

(*f*)

BASS SOLO or
FULL BASSES (and TENORS)

3.'Bring me flesh, and bring me wine, Bring me pine - logs hi - ther:

(Ped.)

Thou and I will see him dine, When we bear them thi - ther.'

(CHOIR and ACCOMPT.)

S. A.

Page and mon-arch, forth they went, Forth they went to - ge - ther:

T. B.

to - ge - ther:

Through the rude wind's wild— la - ment— And the bit-ter wea — - ther.

23. Hark! the herald-angels sing

Words by CHARLES WESLEY (1707–88)
and others

F. MENDELSSOHN (1809–47)
V. 3 arranged by DAVID WILLCOCKS

f 1. Hark! the he - rald - an - gels sing— Glo - ry to the new-born King;
mf 2. Christ, by high - est heav'n a - dored, Christ, the ev - er - last - ing Lord,

Peace on earth and mer - cy mild,— God and sin - ners re - con - ciled:
Late in time be - hold him come— Off - spring of a vir - gin's womb:

Joy - ful all ye na - tions rise,— Join the tri - umph of the skies,—
Veiled in flesh the God - head see,— Hail th'in - car - nate *De - i - ty!—

With th'an - gel - ic host pro - claim, Christ is— born in Beth - le - hem.
Pleased as man with man to dwell, Je - sus,— our Em - ma - nu - el.

Unis.   *Verse 3 overleaf*

Org.
f Hark! the he - rald - an - gels sing Glo - ry— to the new - born King.

Org. Ped.

Melody, and harmony for vv. 1 and 2, adapted by W. H. Cummings (1831–1915) from a chorus by Mendelssohn.
Verses 1 and 2 may be sung by unison voices with organ if desired.   *Deity pronounced Dee - ity*
Also available separately (*Five Christmas Carols* arr. David Willcocks)

for Simon Lindley and the choir of St Albans School

24. Jesus child

Words and music by
JOHN RUTTER

1. Have you heard the sto-ry that they're tell-ing 'bout Beth - le-hem,
2. Have you heard the sto-ry of the poor hum-ble shep - herd men,

1. Have you
2. Sit - ting

Also available separately (X244) and in an arrangement for unison voices (U156)

112 Jesus child

25. A New Year carol

*Words anon.

BENJAMIN BRITTEN
(1913–76)

*From *Tom Tiddler's Ground* — Walter de la Mare

Reprinted by permission of Boosey and Hawkes Music Publishers Ltd., London

REFRAIN *(for verses 1 & 2)*

le - vy dew, sing le - vy dew, the wa - ter and the wine; The

se-ven bright gold wires and the bu-gles that do shine.

D.S. %

REFRAIN *(for verse 3)*

rall. molto

le - vy dew, sing le - vy dew, the wa - ter and the wine; The

una corda

se-ven bright gold wires and the bu-gles that do shine.

26. Here we come a-wassailing

English traditional carol
arranged by JOHN RUTTER

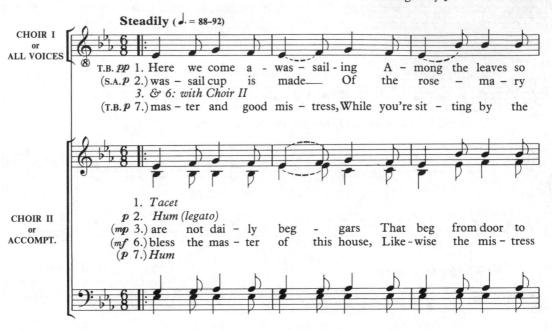

Also available separately (X318)

T.B. *mf* 4. Call up the but–ler of this house, Put
S.A. *f* 5. We have got a lit–tle purse of

v. 3

Year._____

CHOIR II
ONLY   *mf* 4. Aw
       f 5. Ah

Year._____

on his gol–den ring;_____ Let him bring us up_____ a glass of beer, And
stretch–ing lea–ther skin;_____ We want a lit–tle of your mon–ey To

(Aw)
(Ah)

ALL VOICES
(both times)

bet–ter we shall sing: *Love and joy come to you,   And to*
line it well with–in:

(Aw)
(Ah)

to Tom Holme

27. This Christmas night

Words by
MARY WILSON

MALCOLM WILLIAMSON
(*b.* 1931)

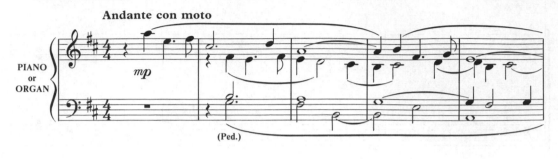

How sweet and clear____ a - bove__ the sounds of war__ The__

mf How__

cla-mo-rous bells are peal - ing their de - light!_____ The

The__

snow_____ To this poor lodg-ing in the bit-ter cold_ Where

Ma – ry kneels_____ with-in the lan-tern glow_____ To watch her

Ba – by ly – ing in the hay,_ And_ think a-bout the won-der of His

ly – ing

birth;_____ And as He sleeps,_____ to fold her hands_____

_____ and pray For peace_____ to come_____ up - on this trou — bled

earth._____

Ped.

i.o.g.D.

28. Hail! Blessed Virgin Mary

Words by
G. R. WOODWARD
(1848–1934)

17th-century Italian carol
arranged by CHARLES WOOD
(1866–1926)

1. Hail! Bless-ed Vir-gin Ma-ry! For so when he did meet thee, Spake migh-ty Ga-bri-el, And thus we greet thee. Come weal, come woe, Our hymn shall nev-er va-ry. Hail! Bless-ed Vir-gin Ma-ry! Hail! Bless-ed Vir-gin Ma-ry!

2. A-ve, a-ve Ma-ri-a! To glad-den priest and peo-ple, The an-ge-lus shall ring from ev-'ry stee-ple, To sound his Vir-gin-birth, Al-le-lu-i-a! A-ve, a-ve Ma-ri-a! A-ve, a-ve Ma-ri-a!

3. Arch-an-gels chant O-san-na, And Ho-ly, Ho-ly, Ho-ly, Be-fore the In-fant born of thee, thou low-ly, Aye - mai-den child of Jo-a-chim and An-na; Arch-an-gels chant O-san-na. Arch-an-gels chant O-san-na.

29. Hush! my dear, lie still and slumber

Words by
ISAAC WATTS
(1674–1748)

French traditional carol
arranged by DAVID WILLCOCKS

Recommended pronunciation of Lullaby = *Loo-la-by.*

2. Sleep, my babe; thy food and rai - ment, House and home, thy friends pro -
4. Soft and ea - sy is thy cra - dle; Coarse and hard thy Sa - viour
6. Lo, he slum - bers in his man - ger, Where the horn-ed ox - en

SOLO ALTO (or A.1 TUTTI)

- vide; All with-out thy care and pay - ment, All thy wants are
lay When his birth-place was a sta - ble And his soft-est
fed; Peace, my dar - ling! here's no dan - ger; Here's no ox a -

well sup - plied.
bed was hay.
near thy bed. Lul - la, lul - la, lul - la,

lul - la - by. Lul - la, lul - la - by.
lul - la, lul - la, lul-la, lul - la, lul - la - by.
lul - la, lul - la - by. Lul - la, lul - la, lul - la - by.

to next page for verses 3 and 5
for verse 7 turn to p. 136

Back to facing page
for verses 4 and 6

★2nd Sop. and 2nd Ten. may be omitted.

30. I saw a maiden

Words 15th century
(adapted)

Old Basque Noël
with refrain by EDGAR PETTMAN
(1865–1943)

SOPRANO
ALTO

1. I___ saw a mai - den___ sit - ten and sing: She
2. This_ ve - ry Lord_ he _ made_ al - le thing: Of
3. There was mick - le me - lo - dy at that _ child - es birth: And
4. An - gels sang that night_ and_ said - en to that child: Now
5. Pray we to that child_ and_ to his mo - ther dear, His

TENOR
BASS

lull - ed a child, a swee - te Lord - - ing.
lord - es the Lord, of king - es the ___ King.
all in hea - ven's bliss, they ma - de mick - le mirth. } Lul -
blest be thou and she, both meek _ and _ mild.
bless - ing to them that mak - en now___ cheer.

lay,_____ lul lay,_____ my _ dear _ son, my _ swee - ing. Lul

- lay, _ lul - lay, _ my _ dear heart, my _ own dear dar - ling.

Alternative version of text (as given in *The University Carol Book*)

1. I saw a maiden sitting and sing,
   She lull'd her child a little Lording.

   Lullay, lullay, my dear son, my sweeting.
   Lullay, lullay, my dear son, my own dear dearing.

2. This very Lord, He made all things,
   And this very God, the King of all Kings.

3. There was sweet music at this child's birth,
   And heaven filled with angels, making much mirth.

4. Heaven's angels sang to welcome the child
   Now born of a maid, all undefiled.

5. Pray we and sing on this festal day,
   That peace may dwell with us alway.

31. Lord of the Dance

Words by
SYDNEY CARTER
(b. 1915)

Melody adapted by SYDNEY CARTER
from a traditional Shaker song,
arranged by DAVID WILLCOCKS

Also available separately from Stainer & Bell

50

mp cresc.

They thought I'd gone – But   I   am the Dance, And I   still   go   on.

mp cresc.

They thought I'd gone – But   I   am the Dance, And I   still   go   on.

mf cresc.

thought   I'd   gone – But   I   am the Dance, And I   still   go   on.

mp cresc.   *f*

thought   I'd   gone – But   I   am the Dance, And I   still   go   on. 'Dance,—

53

S.
A.
f

'Dance,   then,   wher – ev – er you may be,   I   am the Lord   of the
'Dance,   then,—   dance,   then,   I'm the Lord   of the

T.
B.
f

then,

56

Dance,' said— he, 'And I'll lead— you— all, wher – ev – er youmay be, And I'll
Dance,' said— he,

Poco meno mosso

59

mp più legato

S.

lead   you   all   in the Dance,' said he.   Dance,   dance,   dance,   dance,

mp più legato

A.

lead— you   all   in the Dance,' said he.   Dance,   then,   dance,   then,

T.
B.

lead   you   all   in the Dance,' said he.

dance, then, wher – ev – er you may be: 4.I   danced when the

dance, wher – ev – er   you   may   be: 4.I   danced when the

(TENORS and BASSES) *mp* unis.

4.I   danced on a Fri-day When the

sky turned black; It's   hard_ to_ dance_ With the   de - vil on your back. They

whipped and they stripped And they hung me on high, And they   left_ me_ there On a

dim.

cross   to   die.   'Dance,   then,   wher – ev – er you may be:

'Dance,   then,_____   dance,   then,

'Dance,_____   then,

I   am the Lord   of the   Dance,' said_ he,   'And I'll   lead_ you_ all,   wher –

I'm the Lord   of the   Dance,' said_ he,

32. Longfellow's carol

Words by
H. W. LONGFELLOW
(1807–82)

ALLEN PERCIVAL
(*b.* 1925)

Reprinted by permission from *The Galliard Book of Carols*

2. And thought how, as the day had come,
   The belfries of all Christendom
   Had rolled along the unbroken song
   Of peace on earth, good will to men.

3. Till, ringing, singing on its way,
   The world revolved from night to day,
   A voice, a chime, a chant sublime
   Of peace on earth, good will to men.

4. Then from each black accursed mouth
   The cannon thundered in the South,
   And with the sound the carols drowned
   Of peace on earth, good will to men.

5. It was as if an earthquake rent
   The hearth-stones of a continent,
   And made forlorn the households born
   Of peace on earth, good will to men.

6. And in despair I bowed my head;
   'There is no peace on earth,' I said;
   'For hate is strong, and mocks the song
   Of peace on earth, good will to men.'

7. Then pealed the bells more loud and deep:
   'God is not dead; nor doth he sleep!
   The wrong shall fail, the right prevail,
   With peace on earth, good will to men.'

for The King's Singers

33. Il est né le divin enfant
(He is born the divine Christ-child)

Tr. DAVID WILLCOCKS

French traditional carol
arranged by DAVID WILLCOCKS

★*divin* pronounced *di-veen*

© Oxford University Press 1978

*(After Refrain following Verse 4,
go to Coda p. 151)*

Chan - tons tous son a - vè - ne - ment.
Sing we praise to the in - fant mild.

Chan - tons tous son a - vè - ne - ment.
Sing we praise to the in - fant mild.

Chan - tons tous son a - vè - ne - ment.
Sing we praise to the in - fant mild.

VERSES 1 and 3

T. Bar.

f

1. De -puis plus de qua -tre mille ans, Nous le pro - met-taient
3. Une é - ta - ble est son loge -ment, Un peu de paille est
1. More than four thou-sand years on earth, Seers his ad - vent were
3. In a man - ger thou deignst to be, Straw the bed where-on

B.1

mp *p* *mp* *p* *mp* *p*

Né, né, né, né, né, né,
Born, born, born, born, born, born,

B.2

mp

Né,_____ né,_____
Born,_____ born,_____

mf

les pro - phè - tes, De - puis plus de qua - tre mille ans,
sa cou - chet - te, Une é - ta - ble est son loge -ment,
pro - phe - sy - ing; More than four thou-sand years on earth,
thou art ly - ing; In a man - ger thou deignst to be,

mp *p* *simile*

né, né, né, né, né, né,
born, born, born, born, born, born,

né,_____
born,_____

2. Ah, qu'il est beau, qu'il est char-mant, Qu'il est doux, ce di-vin en-fant!
4. O Jé - sus, roi tout puis-sant, Rég-nez sur nous en-tière-ment.
2. *O what beau-ty and charm are thine, O what sweet-ness thou Child di - vine!*
4. *Je-su, King, whom we bow be-fore, Rule our hearts now and ev - er - more.*

La la la la la.

né, né, né, né!
born, born, born, born!

né, né!
born, born!

CODA *(from p. 149)*

est né!
is born!

est né!
is born!

Il est né, il est né, il est né, est né!
He is born, he is born, he is born, is born!

Il est né, il est né, il est né, est né!
He is born, he is born, he is born, is born!

34. Myn lyking

R. R. TERRY
(1865–1938)

Words 15th century

The words of this carol are taken from the Sloane MS. : spellings are unaltered.

Reprinted by permission of J. Curwen & Sons Ltd.

35. I saw three ships
(first tune)

English traditional carol
arranged by DAVID WILLCOCKS

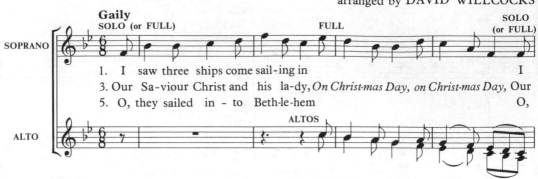

Note: Dynamics are left to the discretion of the conductor.

MELODY

MEN 6. And all the bells_ on earth shall ring   And
SOPS. 7. And all the an-gels in heav'n shall sing *On Christ-mas Day, on Christ-mas Day,* And
MEN 8. And all the souls_ on earth shall sing   And

SEMI-CHORUS

S.
A.

       6. *Ding   dong   ding   dong   ding   dong   ding   dong*
sempre { 7. *Ah* _____
legato { 8. *Aw* _____

T.
B.

       6. *Ding* _____   *dong* _____
sempre { 7. *Ah* _____   *Ah* _____
legato { 8. *Aw* _____   *Aw* _____

all   the bells_   on earth shall ring
all   the an-gels in heav'n shall sing   *On Christ-mas Day in the morn - ing.*
all   the souls_   on earth shall sing

ding   dong   ding   dong   ding   dong   ding - a - dong
Ah _____
Aw _____

ding _____   *dong* _____
Ah _____   *Ah* _____
Aw _____   *Aw* _____

FULL CHORUS

S.
A.

9. Then let us all re - joice a-main! *On Christ-mas Day,_ on Christ-mas Day,_* Then

T.
B.

let us all_ re - joice_ a - main! *On Christ-mas Day in the morn - ing.*

for Sir David Willcocks and the Bach Choir

36. I saw three ships
(second tune)

English traditional carol
arranged by JOHN RUTTER

This arrangement is designed to allow the participation of children, who are taught the melody at the time of performance.

Also available separately

* In the absence of children, this verse may be sung by tenors and basses instead of sopranos and altos.

to Geoffrey Shaw

37. A merry Christmas

Traditional West country carol
arranged by ARTHUR WARRELL
(1883–1939)

Bracketed dynamics are editorial.

got_ some, So bring_some out_ here. Good_ tid - ings_ I_
(We)

Good_

bring_____ To_ you and_ your_ kin;_____ I wish you a mer-ry
(We)

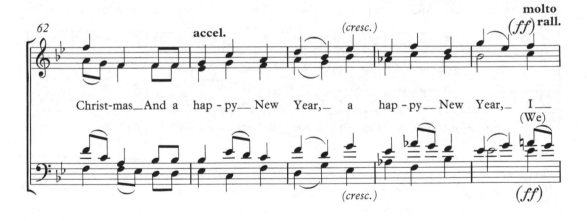

Christ-mas_And a hap-py_ New Year,_ a hap-py_ New Year,_ I_
(We)

accel. *(cresc.)* **molto** *(ff)* **rall.**

(cresc.) *(ff)*

wish you a mer-ry Christ-mas_ And a hap - py_ New Year.

38. I wonder as I wander

Appalachian carol
arranged by JOHN RUTTER

Melody and words collected by John Jacob Niles and reprinted by permission of G. Schirmer Ltd. London

*Recommended pronunciation *loo-la-by.*

39. In the bleak mid-winter

Words by
CHRISTINA ROSSETTI
(1830–94)

GUSTAV HOLST
(1874–1934)

In moderate time

SOPRANO
ALTO

1. In the bleak mid - win - ter Fros-ty wind made moan,___
2. Our God, Heav'n can - not hold___ him Nor___ earth sus - tain;___
3. E - nough for him, whom che - ru - bim Wor-ship night and day,___ A
4. An - gels and arch - an - gels May have ga - thered there,___
5. What___ can I give___ him, Poor as I am?___

TENOR
BASS

Earth stood hard as i - ron, Wa - ter like a stone;
Heav'n and earth shall flee a - way When he comes to reign:
breast - ful of milk___ And a man - ger - ful of hay; E -
Che - ru - bim and se - ra - phim Thronged ___ the___ air; But
If I were a shep - herd I would bring a lamb,

Snow had fal - len, snow on snow, Snow___ on___ snow, The
In the bleak mid - win - ter A sta - ble - place suf - ficed The
- nough for him, whom an - gels Fall___ down be - fore, The
on - ly his mo - ther In her maid - en bliss
If I were a Wise Man I would do my part, — Yet

In the bleak mid - win - ter Long___ a - go.
Lord___ God Al - might - y Je - sus___ Christ.
ox and ass and ca - mel Which___ a - dore.
Wor - shipped the Be - lov - ed With___ a___ kiss.
what I can I give him, Give___ my___ heart.

Reprinted by permission of Oxford University Press and G. & I. Holst Ltd.

to M.A.C.

40. In the bleak mid-winter

Words by
CHRISTINA ROSSETTI
(1830–94)

HAROLD DARKE
(1888–1976)

2. Our God, Heav'n can-not hold him Nor___ earth sus - tain;___

Heav'n and earth shall flee a - way___ When he comes to

reign:___ In the bleak mid - win - ter A

sta - ble - place suf - ficed The Lord___ God Al -

- might - y___ Je - - - - sus Christ.

41. Cradle song

Words by
JOHN RUTTER

Flemish traditional carol
arranged by JOHN RUTTER

1. In Beth - le - hem, all in a sta - ble, Lies a new - born

in - fant mild. By his side a vir - gin mo - ther Watch - es

o'er the ho - ly child. Je - sus, ly - ing in the man - ger,

Comes to us on earth a stran - ger:

Lul - la - by! O

Lul - la,

Lul - la,

This setting may be sung a semitone lower, if preferred.

Also available separately

Melody reprinted by permission of Schott Frères (Brussels).

lul - la - by,____ lul - la,____ lul - la, lul - la - by.

lul - la - by,   lul - la, lul - la, lul - la - by.

lit - tle one sleep;   An - gels round   you   watch   will   keep.

CHOIR I★
(unis.)

f dolce   *mf*

3. 'Ho - san - na   in   the   high - est   hea - ven; Peace, good-will   to

f dolce   *mf*

3. 'Ho - san - na   in   the   high - est;   Peace____   to____

CHOIR II

f dolce   *mf*

Peace____   to

men   on earth.'   Se - ra - phim on high_ in   cho - rus Greet   the

earth.'   Se - ra - phim   on high, se - ra - phim   on high Greet the

f

men_ on earth.'____   Se - ra - phim   in   cho - rus Greet_   the

f

★If preferred, Choir I part may be sung by a solo voice, in which case Choir II should sing 'Ah' or hum.

Sa-viour's joy - ful birth. *Ma-ry's voice, in des - cant blend - ing,*

Sa-viour's joy - ful birth. *Ma-ry's voice, in des - cant*

Joins the heav'n - ly song un - end - ing: Lul - la - by, O

blend - ing, Joins the song un - end - ing: Lul - la - by,

lit - tle one sleep; An - gels round you watch will keep.

lul - la, lul - la - by; An - gels watch will keep.

42. In dulci jubilo

Edited and adapted by
REGINALD JACQUES
(1894–1969)

Old German carol
arranged by R. L. PEARSALL
(1795–1856)

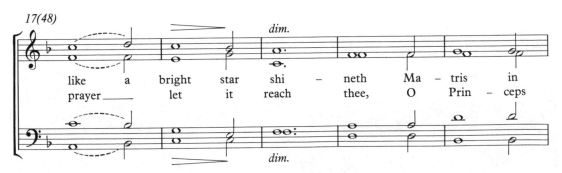

Editors' note: Pearsall's manuscript has been consulted and some small errors in the *Carols for Choirs 1* edition corrected. All resulting discrepancies are identified by footnotes. *(DW and JR)*

*Pearsall marked both verses to be sung by four solo voices, the full choir joining in at bar 25.

† o. in *CC1*

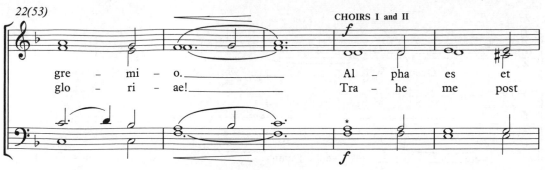

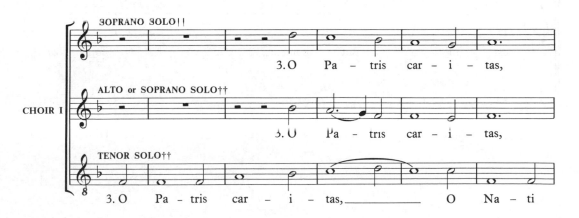

*CCI has an incorrect tenor divisi in this bar.
**CCI has an incorrect alto divisi in this bar.
† o in *CCI* but o· in MS   ††or a few voices   ‡ o· in *CCI*

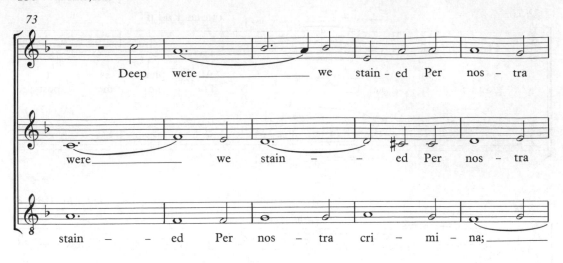

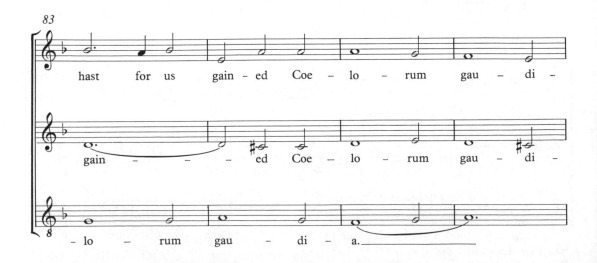

*AA in *CC1*

*or a few voices

108

- ca,_____ There_____ the bells_____ are ring -

There_ the bells are ring - ing In Re - - - -

can - - ti - ca. In

sing - ing, there the bells are ring - - - - - -

SOLO*
p

There the bells are ring - ing In

†

- ing._____ In

SOLO*
p

There_ the bells_____ are

sing - - ing, the bells are ring - ing there In

†o. in *CC1*

*o· in *CC1*

43. Infant holy, infant lowly

Tr. EDITH M. REED

Polish carol
arranged by DAVID WILLCOCKS

Words reprinted by permission of Evans Brothers Ltd

194

44. It came upon the midnight clear

Words by
E. H. SEARS
(1810–76)

English traditional melody
adapted by ARTHUR SULLIVAN
(1842–1900)
V. 4 arranged by DAVID WILLCOCKS

Also available separately (*Six Christmas Hymns* arr. David Willcocks)

© Oxford University Press 1970

gold; When peace shall o'er the earth Its

gold; When peace shall ov - er all the earth Its

Man.

an - cient splen - dours fling, And

an - cient splen - dours fling, And the whole world give__

the whole world Shall__ hear the an - gels sing.

back the song Which now __ the an - gels sing.

Ped.

Tuba

45. Jesus Christ is risen today

Words from *Lyra Davidica* (1708)
and the *Supplement* (1816)

Melody from *Lyra Davidica* (1708)
(altered)
V. 3 arranged by DAVID WILLCOCKS

Verse 3 overleaf

All 1. Jesus Christ is risen today, *Alleluya!*
Our triumphant holy day, *Alleluya!*
Who did once, upon the Cross, *Alleluya!*
Suffer to redeem our loss. *Alleluya!*

All 2. Hymns of praise then let us sing, *Alleluya!*
Unto Christ, our heavenly King, *Alleluya!*
Who endured the Cross and grave, *Alleluya!*
Sinners to redeem and save. *Alleluya!*

Congregation
**(Choir part
overleaf)**
3. But the pains that he endured, *Alleluya!*
Our salvation have procured; *Alleluya!*
Now above the sky he's King, *Alleluya!*
Where the angels ever sing. *Alleluya!*

Also available in *Hymns for Choirs* arr. David Willcocks

*As an alternative to this choir part, the soprano part only may be sung as a descant.

46. The cherry tree carol

English traditional carol
arranged by DAVID WILLCOCKS

1st SOPRANOS

p 3. O then be-spoke Ma - ry, With words both meek and mild,
mf 5. Then bowed down the high-est tree Un - to— our La - dy's hand;

2nd SOPRANOS

V. 3: *pp*
V. 5: *mp* *Ah*_____ *Ah*____

ALTOS

V. 3: *pp*
V. 5: *mp* *Ah*_____ *Ah*____

'Pluck me— one cher-ry, Jo - seph; For— that I am with child.'____
'See,' Ma-ry cried, 'see,— Jo - seph, I have cher-ries at com - mand.'____

TENORS *mp*

*Ah*_____

BARITONES *mf*

4. 'Go to the tree then, Ma - ry, And it— shall bow to thee; And
6. 'O eat your cher-ries, Ma - ry, O— eat— your cher-ries now; O

BASSES *mp*

*Ah*_____

after v. 6: D.C. for v. 7

*Ah*_____

you shall ga - ther cher - ries By— one, by two, by three.'____
eat your cher - ries, Ma - ry, That grow up - on the bough.'____

47. Joy to the world!

Words by
ISAAC WATTS
(1674–1748)

LOWELL MASON (1792–1872)
based on Handel
arranged by JOHN RUTTER

*Tenors and basses sing melody line in unison.

48. King Jesus hath a garden

Tr. G. R. WOODWARD
(1848–1934)

Dutch traditional melody
harmonized by CHARLES WOOD
(1866–1926)

1. King Je - sus hath a gar - den, full of di - vers flow'rs,
Where I go cull - ing po - sies gay, all times and hours.
There naught is heard but Pa - ra - dise bird, Harp, dul - ci - mer, lute,
With cym - bal,

2. The Li - ly, white in blos - som there, is Chas - ti - ty:
The Vi - o - let, with sweet per - fume, Hu - mi - li - ty.

Reprinted from *The Cowley Carol Book* by permission

trump and tym - bal, And the ten - der,— sooth - ing flute; With cym - bal,—

trump and tym - bal, And the ten - der,— sooth - ing flute.—

3. The bonny Damask-rose is known as Patïence:
   The blithe and thrifty Marygold, Obedïence.
   There naught is heard, etc.

4. The Crown Imperial bloometh too in yonder place,
   'Tis Charity, of stock divine, the flower of grace.
   There naught is heard, etc.

5. Yet, 'mid the brave, the bravest prize of all may claim
   The Star of Bethlem—Jesus—blessèd be his Name!
   There naught is heard, etc.

6. Ah! Jesu Lord, my heal and weal, my bliss complete,
   Make thou my heart thy garden-plot, fair, trim and neat.
   That I may hear this musick clear:
   Harp, dulcimer, lute,
   With cymbal, trump and tymbal,
   And the tender, soothing flute.

49. Lo! he comes with clouds descending

Words by
CHARLES WESLEY (1707–88)
and JOHN CENNICK (1718–55)

18th-century English melody
V. 4 arranged by DAVID WILLCOCKS

1. Lo! he__ comes with__ clouds__ de-scend-ing, Once__ for fa-voured
Thou-sand__ thou-sand__ saints__ at-tend-ing Swell__ the tri-umph

sin-ners__ slain;__ Al - le-lu - ia! Al - le-lu - ia!
of__ his__ train:__

Al - le-lu - ia!__ God ap-pears, on__ earth__ to__ reign.

2. Every eye shall now behold him
   Robed in dreadful majesty;
   Those who set at nought and sold him,
   Pierced and nailed him to the tree,
   Deeply wailing (*3 times*)
   Shall the true Messiah see.

3. Those dear tokens of his passion
   Still his dazzling body bears,
   Cause of endless exultation
   To his ransomed worshippers:
   With what rapture (*3 times*)
   Gaze we on those glorious scars!

Harmony for verses 1—3 from *The English Hymnal*

50. Lo, how a Rose e'er blooming

Tr. THEODORE BAKER★

14th-century German melody
harmonized by M. PRAETORIUS
(1571–1621)

1. Lo, how a Rose e'er bloom - ing From
Of Jes - se's lin - eage com - ing As
2. I - sai - ah 'twas fore - told it, The
With Ma - ry we be - hold it, The

ten -der stem hath sprung!
men of old have sung. It came, a flow'-ret bright,—
Rose I have in mind, To show God's love a - right,—
Vir - gin Mo - ther kind.

A - mid the cold of win - ter, When half spent was the night.
She bore to men a Sa - viour, When half spent was the night.

T.
B. } was the

3. O flower, whose fragrance tender
With sweetness fills the air,
Dispel in glorious splendour
The darkness everywhere;
True man, yet very God,
From sin and death now save us,
And share our every load.

*vv. 1 and 2, original text 16th c. German; v. 3, 19th c. German, tr. H. R. Spaeth.

See No. 3 (p. 20) for alternative text.

51a. Coventry carol

Words from the *Pageant of the*
Shearmen and Tailors (15th cent.)

from the *Pageant of the*
Shearmen and Tailors
(1591 version)

After v. 3: repeat refrain

*The original manuscript has F and D in tenor part here.

2. Herod, the king,
   In his raging,
     Chargèd he hath this day
   His men of might,
   In his own sight,
     All young children to slay.

3. That woe is me,
   Poor child for thee!
     And ever morn and day,
   For thy parting
   Neither say nor sing
     By by, lully lullay!

This song is sung by the women of Bethlehem in the play, just before Herod's soldiers come in to slaughter their children.

51b. Coventry carol

Words from the *Pageant of the Shearmen and Tailors* (15th cent.)

from the *Pageant of the Shearmen and Tailors* arranged by MARTIN SHAW (1875–1958)

REFRAIN

Lul - ly, lul - la, thou lit - tle ti - ny child, By by, lul - ly, lul - lay.

End here

1. O sis - ters too, How may we do
2. He - rod, the king, In his rag - ing,
3. That woe is me, Poor child for thee!

For to pre - serve this day This poor young - ling,___ For
Char - ged he hath this day His men of might,___ In
And ev - er morn and day, For thy part - ing Nei - ther

After 3rd verse repeat refrain
Dal 𝄋

whom we do sing, By by, lul - ly lul - lay?
his___ own sight, All young chil - dren to slay.
say___ nor sing By by, lul - ly lul - lay!

This song is sung by the women of Bethlehem in the play, just before Herod's soldiers come in to slaughter their children.

Reprinted by permission of A. R. Mowbray & Co. Ltd.

52. Sir Christèmas

Words anon.
(c. 1500)

WILLIAM MATHIAS
(b. 1934)

Also available separately (X207)
This carol is from *Ave Rex*, a carol sequence by William Mathias (O.U.P.) commissioned
by the Cardiff Polyphonic Choir.

53. Sans Day carol

Cornish traditional carol
arranged by JOHN RUTTER

Arrangement from *Twelve Christmas Carols* (Set 2)

first tree in the green-wood, it was the hol - ly, hol - ly, hol -

- ly! And the first tree in the green-wood, it was the hol -

- ly!

2. Now the hol - ly bears a ber - ry as green as the grass, And

TENORS and BASSES *p ma sonore*

3. Now the hol - ly bears a ber - ry as black as the

coal, And Ma - ry bore Je - sus, who died for us all:

S. A. *Ah*
T. *And*
B. *Ah*

Ma - ry bore Je - sus Christ our Sa - viour for to be, And the

Ah

cresc.

S. *hol - ly, hol -*

first tree in the green-wood, it was the hol - ly,

Ah
A. *Ah*
Ah

(Piano tacet)

Ah

And the first tree in the green-wood, it was the hol - ly!

Ah

ALL VOICES *mf*

4. Now the

hol - ly bears a ber - ry, as blood is it red, Then

54. O come, all ye faithful

(Adeste, fideles)

Tr. F. OAKELEY,
W. T. BROOKE
and others

Words and melody by
J. F. WADE (c. 1711–1786)
arranged by DAVID WILLCOCKS

Note: Verses 1–5 may be sung by unison voices and organ, S.A.T.B. voices and organ, or voices unaccompanied as desired. Verses 3–5 may be omitted. The harmonies used for verses 1–5 are from *The English Hymnal.*

Also available separately (*Five Christmas Carols* arr. David Willcocks)

3. See how the shepherds,
   Summoned to his cradle,
Leaving their flocks, draw nigh with lowly fear;
   We too will thither
   Bend our joyful footsteps:

   O come, etc.

4. Lo! star-led chieftains,
   Magi, Christ adoring,
Offer him incense, gold, and myrrh;
   We to the Christ Child
   Bring our hearts' oblations:

   O come, etc.

5. Child, for us sinners
   Poor and in the manger,
Fain we embrace thee, with awe and love;
   Who would not love thee,
   Loving us so dearly?

   O come, etc.

ALL VOICES

7. Yea, Lord, we greet thee, Born this hap-py morn - ing, Je - su, to thee _ be _ glo — ry giv'n; Word of the Fa - ther, Now in flesh ap - pear -ing: O come, let us a - dore him, O come, let us a - -dore him, O come, let us a - dore him, _ Christ _ the Lord!

55. O come, O come, Emmanuel
(Veni, veni, Emmanuel)

Words 18th century
tr. T. A. LACEY

15th-century French melody★
adapted and arranged by
DAVID WILLCOCKS

Also available separately (*Six Christmas Hymns* arr. David Willcocks)
Congregation should sing sections marked ⌐ ⌐ of verses 1, 2, 4 and 5.
★from a Franciscan Processional (Paris, Bib. Nat., Fonds Latin MS. 10581)

VERSES 2 and 4
TENORS and BASSES

f 2. O come, thou Branch of Jes - se! draw The quar - ry from the li - on's claw; From
f 4. O come, thou Lord of Da - vid's Key! The roy - al door fling wide and free; Safe-

Full Sw. *p*

Ped.

REFRAIN

T.

the dread ca-verns of the grave, From ne-ther hell, thy peo - ple save. Re-
- guard for us the heav'n - ward road, And bar the way to death's a-bode. Re-

B.

the dread ca-verns of the grave, From ne-ther hell, thy peo - ple save. Re-
- guard for us the heav'n - ward road, And bar the way to death's a-bode. Re-

cresc.

f

after v. 2: to next page for v. 3
after v. 4: D.C. for v. 5

-joice! Re-joice! Em - ma - nu - el Shall come to thee, O Is - ra - el.

-joice! Re-joice! Em - ma - nu - el Shall come to thee, O Is - ra - el.

after v. 2: to next page for v. 3
after v. 4: D.C. for v. 5

VERSE 3

mf SOPRANOS and ALTOS

3. O come, O come, thou Day - spring bright! Pour on our souls thy heal - ing light; Dis-

Ch. flutes *p*

(Man.)

S.

cresc.

REFRAIN *f*

- pel the long night's lin - g'ring gloom, And pierce the sha-dows of ___ the tomb. Re -

A.

cresc.

f

- pel the long night's lin - g'ring gloom, And pierce the sha-dows of ___ the tomb. Re -

cresc.

f

Back to p. 231 for v. 4

Em - ma - nu - el Shall come to thee, O Is - ra - el.

- joice! Re - joice! Em - ma - nu - el Shall come to thee, O Is - ra - el.

- joice! Re - joice! Em - ma - nu - el Shall come to thee, O Is - ra - el.

Back to p. 231 for v. 4

56. O little one sweet

Tr. PERCY DEARMER

Old German melody★
harmonized by J. S. BACH
(1685–1750)

1. O little one sweet, O little one mild, Thy Father's
   purpose thou hast fulfilled; Thou cam'st from heav'n to
   mortal ken, Equal to be with us poor
   men, O little one sweet, O little one mild.

2. O little one sweet, O little one mild, With joy thou
   hast the whole world filled; Thou camest here from
   heav'n's domain, To bring men comfort in their
   pain, O little one sweet, O little one mild.

3. O little one sweet, O little one mild,
   In thee love's beauties are all distilled;
   Then light in us thy love's bright flame,
   That we may give thee back the same,
   O little one sweet, O little one mild.

4. O little one sweet, O little one mild,
   Help us to do as thou hast willed.
   Lo, all we have belongs to thee!
   Ah, keep us in our fealty!
   O little one sweet, O little one mild.

★Words and melody first appeared in Samuel Scheidt's *Tablaturbuch* (1650) and may have been written by him.

57. O little town of Bethlehem

Words by
PHILLIPS BROOKS
(1835–93)

English traditional melody
arranged by
R. VAUGHAN WILLIAMS (1872–1958)
and (V. 4) THOMAS ARMSTRONG (b. 1898)

1. O lit-tle town of Beth-le-hem, How still we see thee lie!
2. O morn-ing stars, to-ge-ther Pro-claim the ho-ly birth,
3. How si-lent-ly, how si-lent-ly, The won-drous gift is giv'n!

A-bove thy deep and dream-less sleep The si-lent stars go by.
And prai-ses sing to God the King, And peace to men on earth;
So God im-parts to hu-man hearts The bless-ings of his heav'n.

Yet in thy dark streets shin — eth The e-ver-last-ing light;
For Christ is born of Ma-ry; And, gath-ered all a-bove,
No ear may hear his com — ing; But in this world of sin,

The hopes and fears of all the years Are met in thee to-night.
While mor-tals sleep, the an-gels keep Their watch of wond-'ring love.
Where meek souls will re-ceive him, still The dear Christ en-ters in.

Descant reprinted by permission of The Royal School of Church Music
Arrangement reprinted from the English Hymnal by permission of Oxford University Press.

For alternative tune by Walford Davies, see p. 382.

58. Of the Father's heart begotten

(Corde natus ex Parentis)

Words by PRUDENTIUS
(*c.* 348–413)
tr. R. F. DAVIS

Melody from *Piae Cantiones* (1582)
arranged by DAVID WILLCOCKS

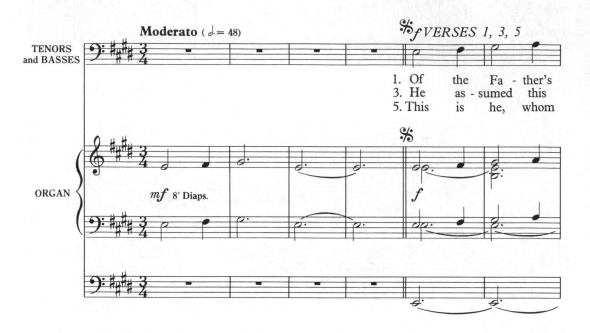

Also available separately (E100)

He is Al - pha: from that Foun - tain   All that is and hath been
That the race from dust cre - a - ted   Might not per - ish ut - ter -
This is he of old re - veal - ed   In the page of pro - phe-

flows;   He is O - me - ga, of all_____ things   Yet to
- ly,   Which the dread- ful Law had sen - - - - tenced   In the
- cy;   Lo! he comes, the pro-mised Sa - - - - viour;   Let the

after vv. 1 and 3: straight on for vv. 2 and 4
after v. 5: to p. 239 for v. 6

come the mys - tic Close,
depths of hell to lie,   *Ev - er - more and ev - er - more._____*
world his prais - es cry!

VERSES 2, 4

SOPRANOS (and ALTOS)

2. By his word was all cre - a - ted; He com-mand - ed and _ 'twas
4. O how blest that won-drous birth - day, When the Maid the curse _ re-

Man. *mf* 8', 4' flutes

done;   Earth and sky and bound-less o - cean,   U - ni - verse of
-trieved, Brought to birth man-kind's sal - va - tion,   By the Ho - ly

three _ in one,   All that sees the moon's soft ra - - - -diance,
Ghost _ con-ceived; And the Babe, the world's Re - deem - - - - er,

D.S. for vv. 3 and 5

All that breathes be - neath the sun,   *Ev - er - more and ev - er - more._*
In her lov - ing arms re - ceived,

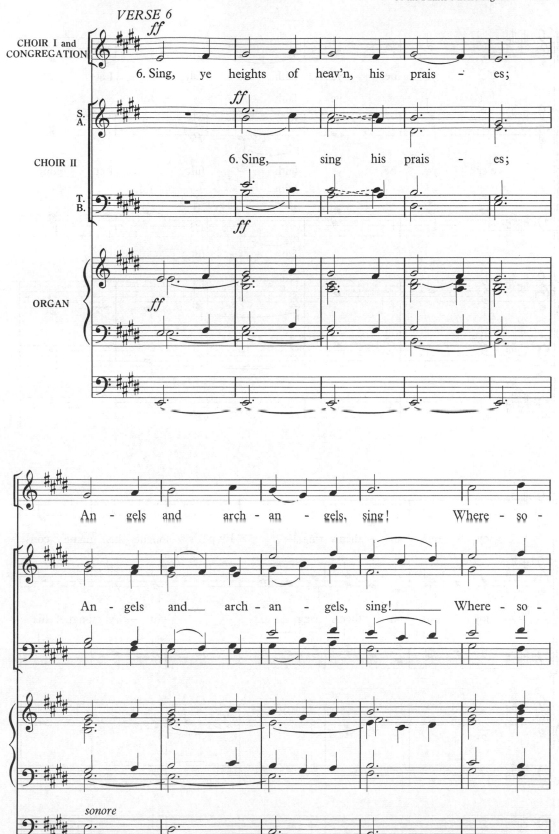

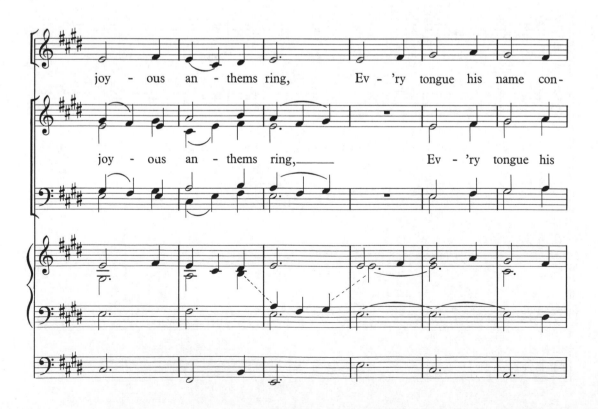

59. Sussex carol

English traditional carol
arranged by DAVID WILLCOCKS

VERSE 1: SOPRANOS (and ALTOS)
VERSE 2: TENORS and BASSES

f 1. On Christ - mas night   all
mf 2. Then why   should men   on

V. 1: T. & B.
V. 2: S. (and A.)

Christ - ians sing,   To hear   the news the an - gels bring,   On
earth be so sad,   Since our   Re - deem - er made   us glad,   Then

Christ - mas night   all   Christ - ians sing,   To hear   the news the
why   should men   on   earth be so sad,   Since our   Re - deem - er

Also available separately (X75)

Melody and words reprinted by permission of Ursula Vaughan Williams

1st time (v. 1)

SOPRANOS (and ALTOS)

an - gels bring— News   of   great joy,__news of__great mirth,

made   us glad?

1st time (v. 1)

ALL VOICES

News   of   our   mer - ci - ful__King's birth.

2nd time (v. 2)

(Voices unaccompanied)

S.
A.

p

When   from   our   sin   he   set   us   free,__

T.
B.

p Organ tacet

All   for__   to   gain our li - ber - ty?

mf

Sussex carol

CHOIR I (melody)

3. When sin de-parts be-fore his grace, Then life and health come

CHOIR II

1st time *mf* Ah
2nd time *p*

(Voices unaccompanied)

1st time   2nd time   *cresc.*

in its place, When in its place; An - gels and men with joy may

cresc.
An - gels and men with

cresc.

sing,   All   for   to   see the new-born King.

joy may sing,   All for to   see the new-born King.

Gt.

Full Sw.

60. The twelve days of Christmas

English traditional carol★
arranged by JOHN RUTTER

Adapted from the arrangement in *Eight Christmas Carols* (Set 2).
Audience may sing melody line during sections marked ⌐ ¬.

★ Melody for "Five gold rings" added by Frederic Austin, and reproduced by
permission of Novello & Co. Ltd.

fourth day of Christ-mas my true love sent to me Four call-ing birds,

three French hens, two tur-tle doves and a par-tridge in a pear

tree. On the fifth day of Christ-mas my true love sent to me

eighth day of Christ-mas my true love sent to me   Eight maids a - milk-ing,

sev'n swans a-swim-ming, six geese a - lay-ing, five gold rings,

four call - ing birds, three French hens, two tur - tle doves and a

par - tridge in a pear tree.   On the ninth day of Christ-mas my

true love sent to me   Nine la - dies danc-ing, eight maids a-milk-ing,

sev'n swans a-swim-ming, six geese a - lay-ing,   five   gold

tree. On __ th'e-lev'nth day of Christ-mas my true love sent to me 'lev'n __

__ pi - pers pi - ping, ten lords a - leap-ing, nine la - dies danc-ing,

eight maids a - milk-ing, sev'n swans a - swim-ming, six geese a - lay-ing,

five gold _ rings, ___ four _ call-ing birds, three French hens,

molto allargando

two tur-tle doves and a par-tridge in a pear tree.   On the

12   **Maestoso**

twelfth day of Christ - mas my true love sent to me

Maestoso

Tempo I (fast)

61. Once in royal David's city

Words by
C. F. ALEXANDER
(1818–95)

H. J. GAUNTLETT (1805–76)
Vv. 1–5 harmonized by A. H. MANN (1850–1929)
V. 6 arranged by DAVID WILLCOCKS

3. And through all his wondrous childhood
He would honour and obey,
Love, and watch the lowly maiden,
In whose gentle arms he lay;
Christian children all must be
Mild, obedient, good as he.

4. For he is our childhood's pattern,
Day by day like us he grew,
He was little, weak and helpless,
Tears and smiles like us he knew;
And he feeleth for our sadness,
And he shareth in our gladness.

5. And our eyes at last shall see him,
Through his own redeeming love,
For that child so dear and gentle
Is our Lord in heaven above;
And he leads his children on
To the place where he is gone.

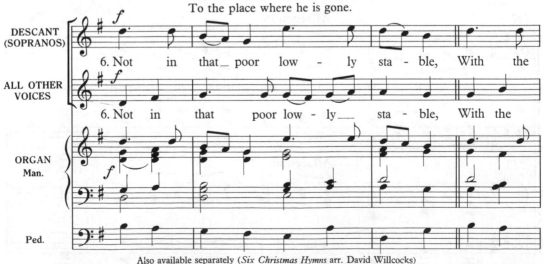

Also available separately (*Six Christmas Hymns* arr. David Willcocks)
* The first verse may be sung by a solo treble.

62. Once, as I remember

Words by
G. R. WOODWARD
(1848–1934)

17th-century Italian carol
arranged by CHARLES WOOD
(1866–1926)

1. Once, as I re-mem-ber, At the time of Yule,
2. Near as man was a-ble, On my knee fell I,
3. Ox and ass a-round him, Court-ier-like, did stand:
4. E-v'ra-mong and o'er us An-gel-quire 'gan sing

Af-ter mid-De-cem-ber, When it blow-eth cool,
In the Beth-lem sta-ble Where the babe did lie,
Fair white li-nen bound him, Spun by Ma-ry's hand,
An-ti-phons in cho-rus To the new-born King.

I o'er-heard a Mo-ther Was a-sing-ing 'Sweet Je-su,
And the Vir-gin-mo-ther Was a-sing-ing 'Sweet Je-su,
While the Vir-gin-mo-ther Was a-sing-ing 'Sweet Je-su, La-lul-lay-
Then the Vir-gin-mo-ther Fell a-sing-ing 'Sweet Je-su,

-lu,____ La-lul-lay-lu,____ La-lul-lay-lu, Lul-lay la-lu.'

Words reprinted from *The Italian Carol Book* by permission of The Faith Press Ltd.

63. Out of your sleep

Words 15th century

RICHARD RODNEY BENNETT
(*b.* 1936)

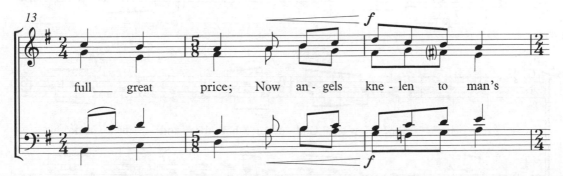

No. 2 of *Five Carols*, reprinted by permission of Universal Edition

64a. Personent hodie

Words from
Piae Cantiones
(1582)

German, 1360
arranged by GUSTAV HOLST
(1874–1934)

For English words, see p. 268.
'Bethlehem adeunt' has been substituted for 'Parvulum inquirunt' (which may well be
a clerical error since no similar repetition of words is to be found in the other verses.)

Reprinted by permission of J. Curwen & Sons Ltd.

64b. Sing aloud on this day!

(Personent hodie)

Tr. JOHN A. PARKINSON

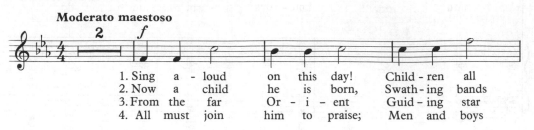

Moderato maestoso

1. Sing a - loud on this day! Child - ren all
2. Now a child he is born, Swath - ing bands
3. From the far Or - i - ent Guid - ing star
4. All must join him to praise; Men and boys

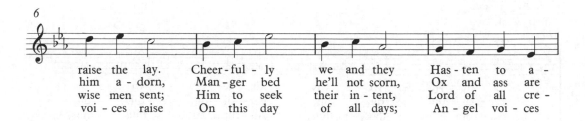

raise the lay. Cheer - ful - ly we and they Has - ten to a -
him a - dorn, Man - ger bed he'll not scorn, Ox and ass are
wise men sent; Him to seek their in - tent, Lord of all cre -
voi - ces raise On this day of all days; An - gel voi - ces

- dore thee, Sent from high - est glo - ry, For us born,
near him; We as Lord re - vere him, And the vain,
- a - tion; Kneel in a - do - ra - tion. Gifts of gold,
ring - ing, Christ - mas ti - dings bring - ing. Join we all,

born, born, For us born, born, born, For us born
vain, vain, And the vain, vain, vain, And the vain
gold, gold, Gifts of gold, gold, gold, Gifts of gold,
all, all, Join we all, all, all, Join we all,

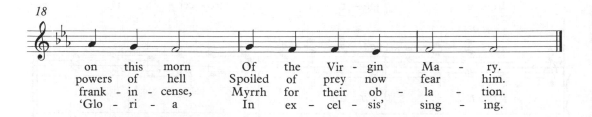

on this morn Of the Vir - gin Ma - ry.
powers of hell Spoiled of prey now fear him.
frank - in - cense, Myrrh for their ob - la - tion.
'Glo - ri - a In ex - cel - sis' sing - ing.

65. Past three a clock

Words by
G. R. WOODWARD
(1848–1934)

English traditional carol
harmonized by CHARLES WOOD
(1866–1926)

SOPRANO
ALTO

Past three a clock, And a cold fros-ty morn – ing: Past three a clock; Good

TENOR
BASS

Fine

mor-row, mas-ters all!

1. Born is a ba – by, Gen-tle as may be,
2. Se-raph quire sing – eth, An-gel bell ring-eth:

Son of th'e-ter – nal Fa-ther su-per-nal.
Hark how they rime it, Time it, and chime it.

Past three a clock,

3. Mid earth rejoices
   Hearing such voices
   Ne'ertofore so well
   Carolling *Nowell.*
   Past three a clock, etc.

4. Hinds o'er the pearly
   Dewy lawn early
   Seek the high stranger
   Laid in the manger.
   Past three a clock, etc.

5. Cheese from the dairy
   Bring they for Mary,
   And, not for money,
   Butter and honey.
   Past three a clock, etc.

6. Light out of star-land
   Leadeth from far land
   Princes, to meet him,
   Worship and greet him.
   Past three a clock, etc.

7. Myrrh from full coffer,
   Incense they offer:
   Nor is the golden
   Nugget withholden.
   Past three a clock, etc.

8. Thus they: I pray you,
   Up, sirs, nor stay you
   Till ye confess him
   Likewise, and bless him.
   Past three a clock, etc.

The refrain *Past three a clock* is old, but the other words are by G.R.W. The tune is *London Waits,* from
W. Chappell's *Popular Music of the Olden Time.*

Reprinted from *The Cambridge Carol Book* by permission

66. Quelle est cette odeur agréable?

(Whence is that goodly fragrance flowing?)

Vv. 1–3 tr. A. B. RAMSAY
V. 4 tr. DAVID WILLCOCKS

French traditional carol
arranged by DAVID WILLCOCKS

English words of vv. 1—3 reprinted by permission of the Master and Fellows of Magdalene College, Cambridge

Also available separately (X209)

67. Quem pastores laudavere

(Shepherds left their flocks a-straying)

Tr. IMOGEN HOLST

14th-century German carol
arranged by JOHN RUTTER

English words reprinted by permission of G. & I. Holst Ltd.

Also available separately (X211)

15

mf dim. *p*

Na - - tus est___ rex glo - - ri - ae.
'Christ___ is born___ in Beth - le - hem.'

mf dim. *p*

17
S. A. *p*

Ah___   Ah___

T. and B. *mp*

2. Ad quem ma - gi am - bu - la - bant, Au - rum, thus,__ myrr-
2. *Wise men came from far,__ and saw him: Knelt__ in hom - age*

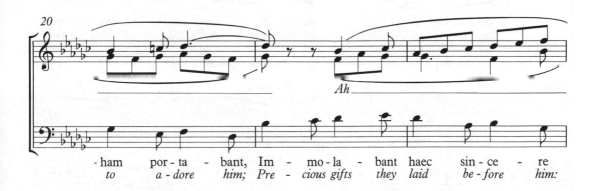

20

Ah___

- ham por - ta - bant, Im - mo - la - bant haec sin - ce - re
to a - dore him; Pre - cious gifts they laid be - fore him:

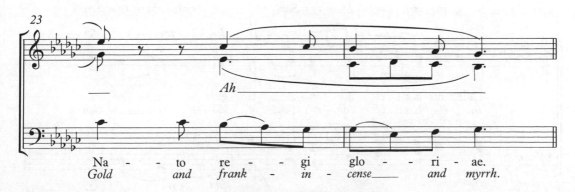

23

Ah___

Na - - to re - - gi glo - - ri - ae.
Gold and frank - in - cense___ and myrrh.

Note: v. 2 may be sung by three solo voices.

Note: Choir I part in v. 3 may be sung by a solo voice, in which case Choir II should sing "*Ah*"

68. Birthday carol

Words adapted from Luke 2

Words and music by
DAVID WILLCOCKS

†Children and/or Audience join in (optional)

Also available separately (X249)

VERSES 2, 4, AND 6

2. Shep-herds a - bi - ding   in the field,   Al - le - lu -
4. 'Ti - dings of   joy to   you I   bring,'
6. A host of   an - gels   fill'd the   sky,

To them God's   glo - ry   was re - veal'd.
- ia, 'To - day is   born a   heav'n-ly King.'   Al - le - lu - ia.
Thus sing-ing   praise to   God on   high:

Glo - ri-a,   Glo - ri - a
Glo - ri-a, Glo - ri - a   in ex - cel-sis,   Glo - ri-a,   Glo - ri - a
Glo - ri-a,   Glo - ri - a
Glo - ri-a,   Glo - ri - a   in ex - cel-sis,   Glo - ri-a,   Glo - ri - a

back to p. 278
for vv. 4 and 6

(to next page
for verse 7)

back to p. 278
for vv. 4 and 6

69. O Queen of heaven

Words 15th century

TIMOTHY ROGERS
(b. 1961)

VERSE 1: SOPRANO (Solo or Semi-chorus)
VERSE 2: TENOR (Solo or Semi-chorus)

Available separately from Stainer & Bell Ltd.

70. See amid the winter's snow

Words by
E. CASWALL
(1814–78)

JOHN GOSS (1800–80)
arranged by DAVID WILLCOCKS

The harmonizations used for the refrain in verses 1, 3, and 4 are Goss's own.

CHOIR I
(and/or
Congregation)

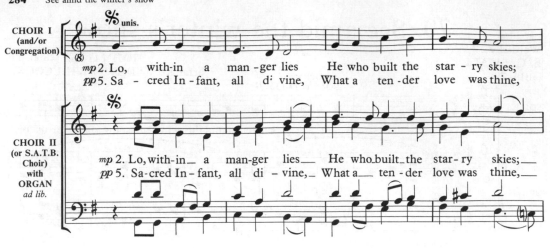

CHOIR II
(or S.A.T.B.
Choir)
with
ORGAN
ad lib.

mp 2. Lo,   with-in   a   man-ger lies   He who built the   star - ry skies;
pp 5. Sa - cred In - fant, all   di - vine,   What a   ten -der   love was thine,

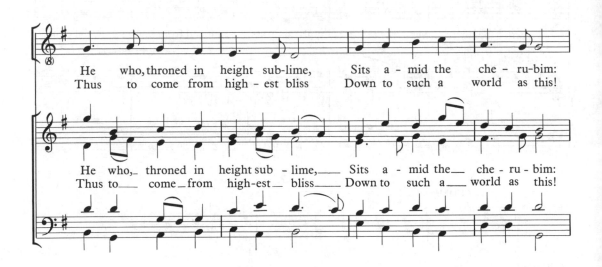

He   who, throned in   height sub-lime,   Sits a - mid the   che - ru-bim:
Thus   to   come from high - est bliss   Down to   such a   world as this!

Hail,   thou ev - er - bless-ed morn! Hail,   re-demp-tion's hap - py   dawn!

after verse 5: to page 287 for last verse

Sing through all Je - ru - sa-lem, Christ is born in Beth - le - hem.

Sing_ through all_ Je - ru - sa - lem,_ Christ_ is born_in Beth - le - hem.

Je - ru - sa - lem,_ Christ is born in Beth - le - hem.

SOPRANOS

3. Say, ye ho - ly shep - herds, say What your joy-ful news to-day;

ALTOS 1 and 2 (or S. 2 and A.)

3. Say, ye ho- ly shep-herds, say_ What your joy - ful news to - day;

Where - fore have ye left your sheep On the lone - ly moun-tain steep?

Where - fore have ye left your sheep On the lone - - ly moun-tain steep?

S. A. CHORUS

Hail, thou ev - er - bless - ed morn! Hail, re-demp-tion's hap - py_ dawn!

T. B. *ƒ* (Organ *ad lib.*)

Sing through all Je - ru - sa - lem,_ Christ is born in Beth - le - hem.

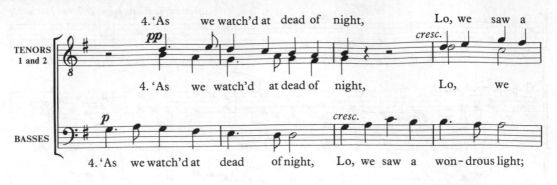

4. 'As we watch'd at dead of night, Lo, we saw a

TENORS
1 and 2

4. 'As we watch'd at dead of night, Lo, we

BASSES

4. 'As we watch'd at dead of night, Lo, we saw a won-drous light;

won-drous light; An - gels sing-ing, Told us of the Sa - viour's birth.'

saw a won-drous light;— An - gels sing-ing of the Sa - viour's birth.'

An - gels sing-ing "Peace on earth" Told us of the Sa - viour's birth.'

CHORUS
S.

A.

Hail, thou ev - er - bless - ed morn! Hail, re-demp-tion's hap - py— dawn!

T.

B. (Organ *ad lib.*)

Dal 𝄋 (p. 284) for verse 5

Sing through all Je - ru - sa - lem,— Christ is born in Beth - le - hem.

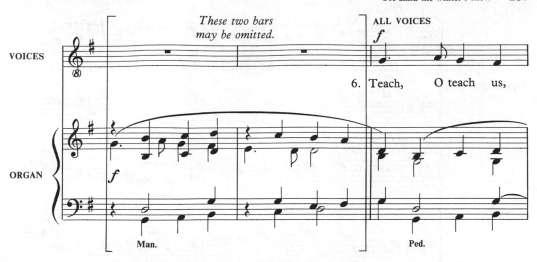

VOICES

These two bars may be omitted.

ALL VOICES

6. Teach, O teach us,

ORGAN

Man.

Ped.

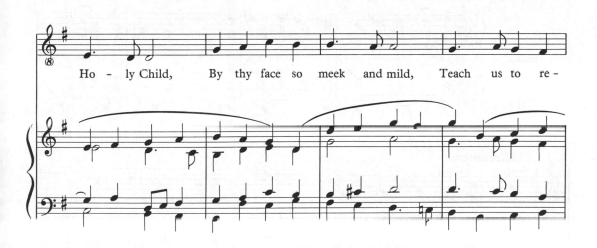

Ho — ly Child, By thy face so meek and mild, Teach us to re-

-sem — ble thee, In thy sweet hu — mi — li -ty:

for JoAnne

71. Mary's lullaby

Words and music by
JOHN RUTTER

Also available separately (X272)

72. Star carol

Words and music by
JOHN RUTTER

Children may join in the melody of the refrain, which is intended to be taught at the time of the performance.

Also available separately (X233) and in an arrangement for unison voices (U153)

10(31)

wor-ship at his cra - dle,   Hur-ry   to Beth – le-hem __ and see the son __ of
King is come to save __ us,   Hur-ry   to Beth – le-hem __ and see the son __ of

A REFRAIN (children join in)
ALL VOICES

13(34)

Ma – ry!   See his star   shin-ing bright
Ma – ry!'

17(38)

In   the sky this __ Christ-mas Night!   Fol-low me   joy-ful-ly;

21(42) *mf* lightly

Hur - ry   to   Beth - le - hem___ and see the son___ of   Ma - ry!

mf lightly
Ww.

mf

2nd time only

p

24 **B** ⌜*1st time*   ⌜*2nd time*

B ⌜*1st time*   ⌜*2nd time*

mf

tr~~~

p dolce

47 **C** *p dolce e legato*

S.

3. See,   he   lies   in   his   mo-ther's ten-der keep - ing;   Je - sus Christ in her

A. *p dolce e legato*

Ah___

T. *p dolce e legato*

Ah___

Piano *p dolce e legato*

B.

Ah___   Ah___

50

lov-ing arms a-sleep.   Shep-herds poor, come to wor-ship and a-dore__ him,

Ah_____   Ah_____

Ah_____   Ah_____

Ah_____

53   Of-fer   their hum-ble gifts__ be-fore the son__ of   Ma - ry.

Ah_____
—   Ah_____

Ah_____
—   Ah_____

p

56   **D** *REFRAIN*
p legato

See   his   star   shin-ing bright   In   the   sky this__

p legato   **D**

Christ-mas Night!__ Fol-low me__ joy-ful-ly;__ Hur-ry to Beth - le - hem__

__ and see the son__ of Ma - ry!

E ALL VOICES

4. Let us all pay our hom-age at the man - ger,

80

In the sky this Christ-mas Night! Fol - low me joy - ful - ly;

84 **G** *mf* — cresc.

Hur - ry to Beth - le - hem and see the son of Ma - ry,

G *mf*

Poco largamente

87 *f* CHILDREN — cresc. **rall** *ff*

Hur - ry to Beth - le - hem and see the son of Ma - ry!

S. A. *f*

Hur - ry to Beth - le - hem and see the son of Ma - ry!

T. B.

Poco largamente

cresc. **rall.** *ff*

8ve

8ve

73. Shepherds, in the field abiding

(Angels, from the realms of glory)

Words by
G. R. WOODWARD
(1848–1934)

French traditional melody
arranged by DAVID WILLCOCKS

1. Shep-herds, in the field a-bid-ing, Tell us, when the se-raph bright Greet-ed you with won-drous tid-ing, What ye saw and heard that night. Glo - - - - - - - - - ri - a
2. We be-held (it is no fa-ble) God in-car-nate, King of bliss, Swathed and cra-dled in a sta-ble, And the an-gel-strain was this: Glo - - - - - - - - - ri - a

3. Quiristers on high were singing
   Jesus and his virgin-birth;
   Heav'nly bells the while a-ringing
   'Peace, goodwill to men on earth.'
   Gloria, etc.

4. Thanks, good herdmen; true your story;
   ★Have with you to Bethlehem:
   Angels hymn the King of Glory;
   Carol we with you and them.
   Gloria, etc.

★Have with you = I am ready to go with you.

ANGELS, FROM THE REALMS OF GLORY
(alternative text)

1. Angels, from the realms of glory,
   Wing your flight o'er all the earth;
   Ye who sang creation's story
   Now proclaim Messiah's birth:
   †*Gloria in excelsis Deo.*

2. Shepherds, in the field abiding,
   Watching o'er your flocks by night,
   God with man is now residing;
   Yonder shines the Infant Light:
   Gloria in excelsis Deo.

3. Sages, leave your contemplations;
   Brighter visions beam afar;
   Seek the great Desire of Nations;
   Ye have seen his natal star:
   Gloria in excelsis Deo.

4. Saints before the altar bending,
   Watching long in hope and fear,
   Suddenly the Lord, descending,
   In his temple shall appear:
   Gloria in excelsis Deo.

5. Though an infant now we view him,
   He shall fill his Father's throne,
   Gather all the nations to him;
   Every knee shall then bow down:
   Gloria in excelsis Deo.

†*ORIGINAL REFRAIN*

Come and worship
   Christ, the new-born King;
Come and worship,
   Worship Christ, the new-born King.

J. MONTGOMERY (1771–1854)

74. The Infant King

Words by
S. BARING-GOULD
(1834–1924)

Basque Noël
arranged by DAVID WILLCOCKS

Dolce e legato (♪ = 108)

SOPRANO

1. *Sing lul - la - by!* Lul - la - by ba - by, now re -
2. *Sing lul - la - by!* Lul - la - by ba - by, now a -
3. *Sing lul - la - by!* Lul - la - by ba - by, now a -
4. *Sing lul - la - by!* Lul - la - by! is the babe a -

ALTO

1. Lul - la - by ba - by, now__ re - clin -
2. Lul - la - by ba - by, now__ a - sleep -
3. Lul - la - by ba - by, now__ a - doz -
4. Lul - la - by! is the babe__ a - wak -

TENOR

1. Lul - la - by ba - by, now__ re - clin -
2. Lul - la - by ba - by, now__ a - sleep -
3. Lul - la - by ba - by, now__ a - doz -
4. Lul - la - by! is the babe__ a - wak -

BASS

1. Lul - la - by ba - by, now re - clin -
2. Lul - la - by ba - by, now a - sleep -
3. Lul - la - by ba - by, now a - doz -
4. Lul - la - by! is the babe a - wak -

3

(Soprano)

- clin - ing, *Sing lul - la - by!* Hush, do not wake the In - fant
- sleep - ing, *Sing lul - la - by!* Hush, do not wake the In - fant
- doz - ing, *Sing lul - la - by!* Hush, do not wake the In - fant
- wak - ing? *Sing lul - la - by!* Hush, do not stir the In - fant

(Alto)

- - ing, *Sing lul - la - by!* Hush, do not wake__ the In - fant
- - ing, *Sing lul - la - by!* Hush, do not wake__ the In - fant
- - ing, *Sing lul - la - by!* Hush, do not wake__ the In - fant
- - ing? *Sing lul - la - by!* Hush, do not stir __ the In - fant

(Tenor)

- - ing, *Sing lul - la - by!* Hush, __ do not wake__ the In - fant
- - ing, *Sing lul - la - by!* Hush, __ do not wake__ the In - fant
- - ing, *Sing lul - la - by!* Hush, __ do not wake__ the In - fant
- - ing? *Sing lul - la - by!* Hush, __ do not stir __ the In - fant

(Bass)

- - ing, *Sing lul - la - by!* Hush, do not wake the In - fant
- - ing, *Sing lul - la - by!* Hush, do not wake the In - fant
- - ing, *Sing lul - la - by!* Hush, do not wake the In - fant
- - ing? *Sing lul - la - by!* Hush, do not stir the In - fant

75. Silent night
(Stille Nacht)

Words by JOSEF MOHR (1792–1848)
tr. anon.

FRANZ GRUBER (1787–1863)
arranged by DAVID WILLCOCKS

Piacevole

p 1. Si - lent night, ho - ly night, All is calm,
1. Stil - le Nacht, hei - li - ge Nacht! Al - les schläft,
* *pp* 3. Si - lent night, ho - ly night, Son of God,
3. Stil - le Nacht, hei - li - ge Nacht! Got - tes Sohn,

Ah_____ Ah_____

all is bright;_____ Round yon vir - gin mo - ther and child.
ein - sam wacht_____ Nur das trau - te, hoch - hei - li - ge Paar.
love's pure light;_____ Ra - diance beams from thy ho - ly face,
O wie lacht_____ Lieb' aus dei - nem gött - lich - en Mund,

Ah_____ Ah_____ Ah_____

Ho - ly in - fant so ten - der and mild, Sleep in hea - ven - ly
Hol - der Kna - be im lock - i - gen Haar, Schlaf' in himm - li - scher
With the dawn of re - deem - ing grace, Je - sus, Lord, at thy
Da uns schlägt_____ die ret - ten - de Stund', Christ, in dei - ner Ge -

Ah_____ Ah_____ Ah_____

peace,_____ Sleep_____ in hea - ven - ly peace.
Ruh',_____ Schlaf'_____ in himm - li - scher Ruh'.
birth,_____ Je - sus, Lord, at thy birth.
- burt,_____ Christ,_____ in dei - ner Ge - burt.

Ah_____

*If preferred, A.T.B. may hum in v. 3.

Also available separately (X313)

76. Still, still, still

Tr. MEG PEACOCKE

German carol
arranged by PHILIP LEDGER
(b. 1937)

Also available separately (X284)

37

3. Gross, — gross, — gross, ——— die — Lieb ist — üb – er – gross! ——— Gott
3. *Joy,* — *joy,* — *joy,* ——— *My* — *heart is* — *filled with* — *joy!* ——— *The*

41

hat den — Him-mels – thron ver – las – sen und muss rei – sen auf der — Strass-en.
God of — *love has* *left his* — *throne,* *Made this* — *hum ble* *world his* — *own,* —

45

Gross, — gross, — gross, ——— die — Lieb ist – üb – er – gross! ———
Joy, — *joy,* — *joy,* ——— *My* — *heart is* — *filled with* — *joy!* ———

rall.

77. Lute-book lullaby

Words by
W. BALLET

W. BALLET (17th cent.)
arranged by GEOFFREY SHAW
(1879–1943)

From the MS. *Lute Book* by William Ballet, early seventeenth century, Trinity College, Dublin.

78. Christmas Night

Melody from Arbeau's
Orchésographie (1588)

Words by
JOHN RUTTER

arranged by JOHN RUTTER

VERSE 1: SOPRANOS (and ALTOS)
VERSE 2: TENORS and BASSES

Andante tranquillo (♩. = 48)

VOICES

dolce

p 1. Soft – ly through the win-ter's
mp 2. Shep-herds kneel in ad-o-

ORGAN

dolce e legato

p

p *(rpt. mp)*

Man.

Ped.

8(34)

dark-ness shines a light, Clear and still in Beth-le-hem— on Christ-mas
-ra – tion by— his bed; Se – ra-phim in glo-ry hov-er round his

16(42)

Night Round the sta – ble where a vir – gin mo – ther mild
head. Wise— men, gui – ded by— the lead-ing of— a star, *dim.*

(dim.)
v.2

Man.

23(49)

1st time

Watch-es ov-er Je – sus Christ the ho – ly child.
p Bring him gifts of pre – cious trea – sure from— a –

Ped.

Also available separately (X316)

3. Choirs_ of an-gels sing_ to greet_ his won-drous birth:_ Christ_ our

Lord in hu – man form_ comes down_ to earth._ 'Glo-ry to God_ in

high – est heav'n' their joy – ful strain:_ 'Peace_ on earth, good-will_ to

Lord who sent__ him down__ from heav'n a - bove: Ho - ly

Praise__ the Lord__ who sent__ him down__ from heav'n a - bove:

in - fant, born__ of God__ the Fa - ther's love.

In - fant, born of God the Fa - ther's love.

Ped.

79. Gabriel's message

Words by
S. BARING-GOULD
(1834–1924)

Basque carol
arranged by
DAVID WILLCOCKS

80. Joys seven

English traditional carol
arranged by STEPHEN CLEOBURY
(b. 1948)

The original version of this arrangement (for SSAATTBB with organ) is available separately (X290).

61

see her own son, Je - sus Christ, To read the bi – ble o'er: *To read the bi - ble*

mf

Gt. 8' +
Sw. 8' 4' 2'   *mf*

Ped.

66

o'er, good man: And bless-ed may he be,_____ Both__ Fa-ther, Son, and

o'er,   And   *bless - ed*_____ *may he be,*   Both__   Fa – ther,__
    bless - ed   *may*_____ *he be,*

may he

71   Ho - ly Ghost, To all e-ter - ni - ty.

Son,_____ To all e-ter - ni - ty.

TENORS   *poco f*

5. The next good joy that

Sw.

Sw.

(Ped.)

Ma - ry had, It was the joy of five; To see her own son, Je - sus Christ, To

bring the dead a - live: *To bring the dead a - live, good man: And bless-ed may he*

be,_____   Both__ Fa-ther, Son, and Ho- ly Ghost, To all e - ter - ni-

- ty.   6. The next good joy_ that

81. The first Nowell

English traditional carol
arranged by DAVID WILLCOCKS

Also available separately (*Five Christmas Carols* arr. David Willcocks)

REFRAIN

cold win-ter's night_ that was_ so deep: No - well,_ No - well,_ No-

-well,_ No - well,_ Born is the King_ of Is - ra - el!

SOPRANO
ALTO

(ORGAN)

TENOR
BASS

2. They_ look - ed_ up___ and_ saw_ a_ star,_ Shin-ing
4. This_ star___ drew nigh___ to_ the_ north- west;_ O'er_

in___ the east,_ be - yond___ them_ far;_ And_
Beth - le - hem___ it took___ its_ rest,_ And_

Note: vv. 2 & 4 may be sung by unaccompanied voices.

Note: vv. 3 & 5 may be sung unaccompanied, or with organ, or by unison voices (tenor part) with descant (soprano part) and organ.

82. The holly and the ivy

English traditional carol
arranged by H. WALFORD DAVIES
(1869–1941)

Allegretto
mf SOLO

1. The hol - ly and the i - vy When they are both full grown;
(A boy's voice) 2. The hol - ly bears a blos - som As white as a - ny flower;
(A man's voice) 3. The hol - ly bears a ber - ry As red as a - ny blood;
(A boy's voice) 4. The hol - ly bears a prick - le As sharp as a - ny thorn;
(A man's voice) 5. The hol - ly bears a bark As bitt - 'r as a - ny gall;

DUET

Of all the trees that are in the wood The hol - ly bears the
And Ma - ry bore sweet Je - sus Christ To be our sweet Sa -
And Ma - ry bore sweet Je - sus Christ To do poor sin - ners
And Ma - ry bore sweet Je - sus Christ On Christ-mas Day in the
And Ma - ry bore sweet Je - sus Christ For to re - deem us

crown.
- viour.
good.
thorn.
all. REFRAIN

SOPRANO mf f
O the ris - ing of the sun And the run-ning of the

ALTO mf f 3
O the ris - ing of the sun And the run-ning of the

TENOR mf f 3
O the ris - ing of the sun And the run-ning of the

BASS mf f
O the ris - ing of the sun And the run-ning of the

(For practice only) mf f 3 3

Also available separately (from the RSCM)

© H. Walford Davies 1913

deer,   The playing of the merry organ,   Sweet singing in the choir.

deer,   The playing of the merry organ,   Sweet singing in the choir.

deer,   The playing of the organ,   Sweet singing in the choir.

deer,   The playing of the organ,   Sweet singing in the choir.

sing-ing, sweet sing - - - ing in the choir.

sing-ing, sweet sing - - - ing in the choir.

sing-ing, sweet sing - - - ing in the choir.

sing-ing, sweet sing - - - ing in the choir.

83. Jesus Christ the apple tree

Words from *Divine Hymns or Spiritual Songs*, compiled by
JOSHUA SMITH
(New Hampshire, 1784)

ELIZABETH POSTON
(1905–87)

♩ = 120

VERSE 1: UNISON
VERSE 5: ROUND (optional), entries at *

1. The tree of life my soul hath seen, La-den with fruit and al-ways green: The
5. This fruit doth make my soul to thrive, It keeps my dy-ing faith a-live; This

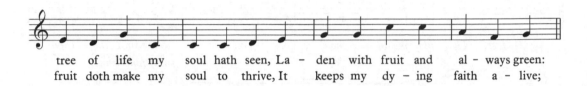

tree of life my soul hath seen, La-den with fruit and al-ways green:
fruit doth make my soul to thrive, It keeps my dy-ing faith a-live;

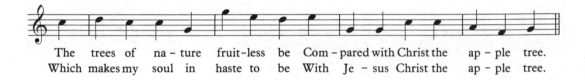

The trees of na-ture fruit-less be Com-pared with Christ the ap-ple tree.
Which makes my soul in haste to be With Je-sus Christ the ap-ple tree.

SSAA unaccompanied or S(S) acc.

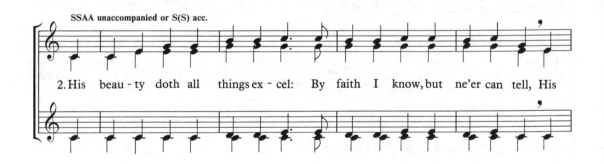

2. His beau-ty doth all things ex-cel: By faith I know, but ne'er can tell, His

beau-ty doth all things ex-cel: By faith I know, but ne'er can tell

cresc.

The glo-ry which I now can see In Je-sus Christ the ap-ple tree.

cresc.

4-PART, or UNISON (acc.)

3. For hap-pi-ness I long have sought, And plea-sure dear-ly
4. I'm wea-ry with my for-mer toil, Here I will sit and

I have bought: For hap-pi-ness I long have sought, And
rest a-while: I'm wea-ry with my for-mer toil, Here

plea-sure dear-ly I have bought: I missed of all; but
I will sit and rest a-while: Un-der the sha-dow

optional ending
last time (acc. only)

now I see 'Tis found in Christ the ap-ple tree.
I will be, Of Je-sus Christ the ap-ple tree.

84. There is no rose

Anon., *c.* 1420
transcribed and edited by
JOHN STEVENS

Note by John Stevens:
From a MS. roll of carols, copied out in the early 15th century and now in the Library of Trinity College, Cambridge; printed by kind permission. The carol begins and ends with the refrain (the alto part is editorial and may be omitted at will); the verses are for soloists. Small accidentals in the refrain are absent from the MS. and may be ignored if desired. The tenor has the tune throughout, and the other voices should be subordinate. The music was intended to be sung unaccompanied.

85. There is a flower

Words by
JOHN AUDELAY (15th cent.)

JOHN RUTTER

Also available separately (X295)

*These three bars may alternatively be sung by 2nd altos.

*sand = gift

*bed = bud

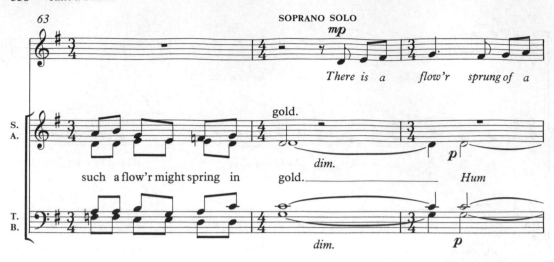

SOPRANO SOLO

There is a flow'r sprung of a

(S.A.) such a flow'r might spring in gold._____ Hum

(T.B.)

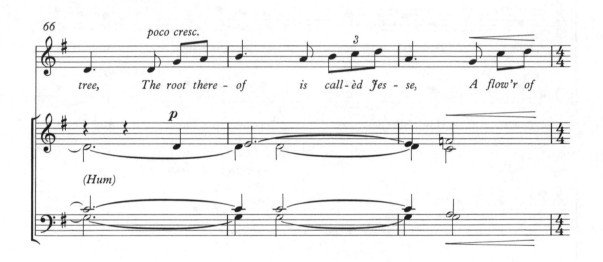

tree, The root there-of is call-èd Jes - se, A flow'r of

(Hum)

price;_____ There is none such in pa - - ra - dise.

(Hum)

86. Rise up, shepherd, and follow

Spiritual
arranged by JOHN RUTTER

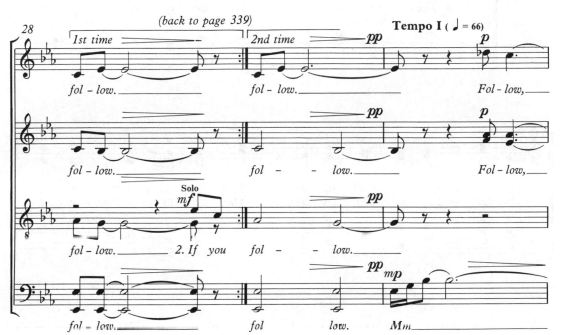

(back to page 339)

87. The truth from above

English traditional carol
arranged by R. VAUGHAN WILLIAMS
(1872–1958)

1. This is the truth__ sent from a - bove,__ The
2. The first thing which __ I do re - late__

truth of God,__ the God __ of love,__ There - fore don't turn__ me__
Is that God__ did man cre - ate; __ The __ next thing which __ to __

from your door, __ But __ heark - en all_____ both__ rich__ and _ poor.
you I'll tell __ Wo - man was made_____ with__ man__ to __ dwell.

3. Thus we were heirs to endless woes,
   Till God the Lord did interpose;
   And so a promise soon did run
   That he would redeem us by his Son.

4. And at that season of the year
   Our blest Redeemer did appear;
   He here did live, and here did preach,
   And many thousands he did teach.

5. Thus he in love to us behaved,
   To show us how we must be saved;
   And if you want to know the way,
   Be pleased to hear what he did say.

Reprinted from *Eight Traditional English Carols* (R. Vaughan Williams) by permission of Stainer & Bell Ltd.

88. This joyful Eastertide

Words by
G. R. WOODWARD
(1848–1934)

Dutch carol
arranged by CHARLES WOOD
(1866–1926)

This joy-ful_Eas-ter-tide,____ A-way with sin and_ sor - - row!
My Love, the_Cru-ci-fied,____ Hath sprung to life this_ mor - - row.

Had Christ, that once was_slain, Ne'er burst his_ three-day pri - son, Our

faith had been_ in vain: But_ now hath Christ a-ris - en,_ a-ris-en, a-ris-en, a-ris - - - en.

2. My flesh in hope shall rest,
   And for a season slumber:
   Till trump from east to west
   Shall wake the dead in number.
   Had Christ, that once, etc.

3. Death's flood hath lost his chill,
   Since Jesus cross'd the river:
   Lover of souls, from ill
   My passing soul deliver.
   Had Christ, that once, etc.

89. The shepherds' farewell
(from *L'enfance du Christ*, Op. 25)

Tr. PAUL ENGLAND

Words and music by
HECTOR BERLIOZ
(1803–69)

Allegretto (♩. = 50) (*v. 3: **Un poco più lento***)

SOPRANO
ALTO

p 1. Thou must leave thy lowly
p 2. Bless-ed Je-sus, we im-
sempre pppp 3. Blest are ye be-yond all

TENOR
BASS

PIANO
or
ORGAN

Oboes

Strings

f

p

Clars.

8

v. 2
(all voices)

dwell-ing, The hum-ble crib, the sta-ble bare, Babe, all mor-tal
-plore thee With hum-ble love and ho-ly fear, In the land that
mea-sure, Thou hap-py fa-ther, mo-ther mild! Guard ye well your

v. 2

(Accompaniment doubles voice parts)

15

v. 3
alto

poco f (*v. 1 only*)

p

babes ex-cel-ling, Con-tent our earth-ly lot to share, Lov-ing
lies be-fore thee, For-get not us who lin-ger here! May the
heav'n-ly trea-sure, The Prince of Peace, the Ho-ly Child! God go

vv. 1
and 2

S.
A.

poco f (*v. 1 only*)

T.
B. 2. May

p

*Verse 3 pppp throughout

90. The three kings

Words★ and music by
PETER CORNELIUS (1824–74)
arranged by IVOR ATKINS
(1869–1953)

Tr. H. N. BATE

★Chorale text by Philipp Nicolai (1556–1608)
†The singers should be placed, if possible, at some distance from the soloist.

Also available separately (OCS 1502)

King; Gold, in - cense, myrrh   are their of - fer - ing.   2. The star shines

Jes - se   tree   now   blow - - eth.

Jes - se   tree   now   blow - - eth.

out___   with   a   stead - fast   ray;   The   kings   to   Beth - le - hem

pp

Of   Ja - cob's   stem   and

pp

make their way,   And there in   wor-ship they bend the__ knee, As   Ma - ry's

p

poco

Da - vid's   line,   For   thee,   my

p

poco

child__   in   her__ lap   they__ see;   Their roy - al   gifts they show to the

p

Bride - groom,   King   di - vine,   My

p

*Tempo markings here and in bar 25 have been added according to the original.

91. Tomorrow shall be my dancing day

English traditional carol
arranged by DAVID WILLCOCKS

Also available separately (X141)

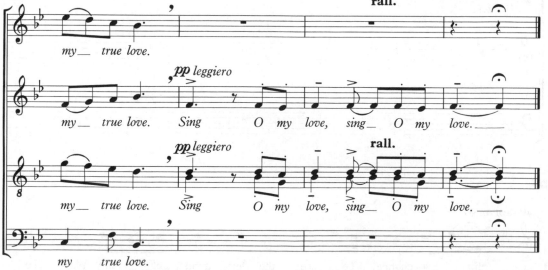

92. Unto us is born a Son

Tr. G. R. WOODWARD

Words and melody from
Piae Cantiones (1582)
arranged by DAVID WILLCOCKS

Also available separately (*Five Christmas Carols* arr. David Willcocks)

*may be sung accompanied, or by unison voices with organ.

Words reprinted from *The Cowley Carol Book* by permission

© Oxford University Press 1961

own-erknow, Be-cra-dled in the__ man-ger, be-cra-dled in the   man-ger.

TENORS and BASSES

3. This did He-rod sore af-fray, And grie-vous-ly be - wil - der,   So he gave the

Full Sw.   *mf* ————————   *f*

Ped.   Man.

word to slay, And   slew the lit - tle   chil - der, and   slew the lit - tle chil - der.

f   *ff*

Ped.

SOPRANOS

4. Of his love and   mer-cy mild   This the Christ-mas sto - ry; And   O that Ma-ry's

p

Man.

*optional, or soprano part as a descant.

93. Up! good Christen folk, and listen

Words by
G. R. WOODWARD
(1848–1934)

Melody from *Piae Cantiones* (1582)
harmonized by G. R. WOODWARD

12(22)

Come a - dore the new - - born___ King:
Show'r - ing bless - ings far_____ and___ wide,

25

Born of___ mo - ther,___ blest__ o'er o - ther,___ *Ex Ma - ri - a*

28

Vir - gi - ne, In a sta - ble ('tis no fa - ble),

31

Chris - tus na - tus ho - - di - e.

The first four bars may be repeated at the end.

94. Wassail song

English traditional carol
arranged by R. VAUGHAN WILLIAMS
(1872–1958)

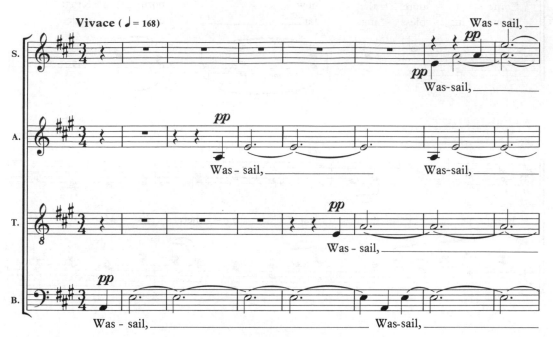

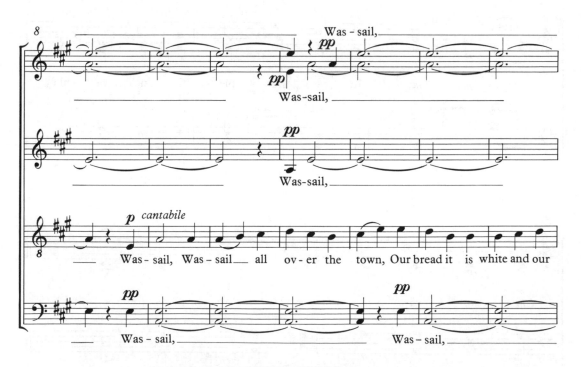

No. 5 of *Five English Folk Songs*

90

S.
A.

pray that your soul — in — heav'n — may rest; — But if — you — do — bring us a —

T.
B.

96   ⋆ff

bowl of the small, — May the De-vil   take but – ler,   bowl — and   all! — Then

102   ⋆ff

here's to the   maid   in the li - ly white smock, Who tripp'd to the   door — and —

108

slipp'd back the — lock; — Who tripp'd to — the — door and — pull'd back the pin, — For to

Was - sail-ers walk in;   Who   tripp'd to — the — door _____

114

let — these jol - ly Was - sail - — - -ers walk in;   and —

⋆It is suggested that *mf* be substituted for *ff* here. *(DW and JR)*

95. Kings of Orient

Words and melody by
J. H. HOPKINS (1820–91)
arranged by DAVID WILLCOCKS

1. We three kings of O-ri-ent are; Bear-ing gifts we tra-verse a-far Field and foun-tain, moor and moun-tain, Fol-low-ing yon-der star: O ____ star of won-der, star of night, Star with roy-al beau-ty bright, West-ward lead-ing,

still pro - ceed - ing, Guide us to thy per - fect light.

(Melchior)
2. Born a king on Bethlehem plain,
   Gold I bring, to crown him again—
   King for ever, ceasing never,
   Over us all to reign:
   O star of wonder, etc.

(Caspar)
3. Frankincense to offer have I;
   Incense owns a deity nigh:
   Prayer and praising, all men raising,
   Worship him, God most high:
   O star of wonder, etc.

('Balthazar)
4. Myrrh is mine; its bitter perfume
   Breathes a life of gathering gloom;
   Sorrowing, sighing, bleeding, dying,
   Sealed in the stone-cold tomb:
   O star of wonder, etc.

(All)
5. Glorious now, behold him arise,
   King, and God, and sacrifice!
   Heav'n sings alleluya,
   Alleluya the earth replies:
   O star of wonder, etc.

Verses 2, 3, and 4 may be sung by three different soloists whilst the choir accompanies, singing *Ah*.

96. What cheer?

Words from RICHARD HILL'S
Commonplace Book (16th cent.)

WILLIAM WALTON
(1902–83)

97. When Christ was born

Words 15th century
(adapted)

REGINALD JACQUES
(1894–1969)

1. When Christ was born of Ma - ry free, In Beth - lem in that
3. This King is come to save his kind, In the scrip - ture
4. Then, dear Lord, for thy great grace, Grant us the bliss to

fair ci - ty, An - gels sung e'er with mirth and glee,
as we find; There-fore this song have we in mind: In ex - cel - sis glo - ri - a.
see thy face, Where we may sing to thy so - lace:

2. Herd-men be-held these an - gels bright—To them ap-pear-ed with great light, And

D.C. for vv. 3 & 4

said, 'God's son is born this night': In ex - cel - sis glo - ri - a.

Words reprinted from *The Oxford Book of Carols* by permission

98. The crown of roses

Words by
A. N. PLESHCHEEV (1825–93)
tr. G. DEARMER

P. I. TCHAIKOVSKY
(1840–93)

Translation from *The Oxford Book of Carols* by permission

3. 'Do you bind ro - ses in ___ your hair?'___ They cried, in scorn, to
'Do you bind ro - ses in your hair?' They cried, in scorn, to
3. 'Do you bind ro - ses in ___ your hair?' They cried, in scorn, to

Je - sus there. The boy said hum - bly: 'Take, I pray, All but the

na - ked thorns a - way.' 4. Then of the thorns they made a crown, And

with rough fin - gers ___ pressed it ___ down, Till on his fore - head fair and

young Red drops of ___ blood ___ like ro - ses sprung. ___

like ro - ses sprung, like ro - ses sprung. ___

99. While shepherds watched their flocks

Words by
NAHUM TATE
(1652–1715)

Este's Psalter (1592)
V. 6 arranged by DAVID WILLCOCKS

1. While shep-herds watched their flocks by night, All seat-ed on the ground, The an-gel of the Lord came down, And glo-ry shone a-round.

2. 'Fear not,' said he (for might-y dread Had seized their troub-led mind); 'Glad ti-dings of great joy I bring To you and all man-kind.

3. 'To you in David's town this day
   Is born of David's line
   A Saviour, who is Christ the Lord;
   And this shall be the sign:

4. 'The heav'nly Babe you there shall find
   To human view displayed,
   All meanly wrapped in swathing bands,
   And in a manger laid.'

5. Thus spake the seraph; and forthwith
   Appeared a shining throng
   Of angels praising God, who thus
   Addressed their joyful song:

Also available separately (*Six Christmas Hymns* arr. David Willcocks)

100. Ye choirs of new Jerusalem

Words by
ST FULBERT of Chartres
(c. 1000)

H. J. GAUNTLETT (1805–76)
V. 6 arranged by DAVID WILLCOCKS

Text in *The English Hymnal*

1. Ye choirs of new Jerusalem,
    Your sweetest notes employ,
   The Paschal victory to hymn
    In strains of holy joy.

2. How Judah's Lion burst his chains,
    And crushed the serpent's head;
   And brought with him, from death's domains,
    The long-imprisoned dead.

3. From hell's devouring jaws the prey
    Alone our Leader bore;
   His ransomed hosts pursue their way
    Where he hath gone before.

4. Triumphant in his glory now
    His sceptre ruleth all,
   Earth, heav'n, and hell before him bow,
    And at his footstool fall.

5. While joyful thus his praise we sing,
    His mercy we implore,
   Into his palace bright to bring
    And keep us evermore.

6. All glory to the Father be,
    All glory to the Son,
   All glory, Holy Ghost, to thee,
    While endless ages run. Alleluya!   Amen.

Translation by R. CAMPBELL (1814–1868)

Text in *Hymns Ancient and Modern*

1. Ye choirs of new Jerusalem,
    Your sweetest notes employ,
   The Paschal victory to hymn
    In strains of holy joy.

2. For Judah's Lion bursts his chains,
    Crushing the serpent's head;
   And cries aloud through death's domains
    To wake th' imprisoned dead.

3. Devouring depths of hell their prey
    At his command restore;
   His ransomed hosts pursue their way
    Where Jesus goes before.

4. Triumphant in his glory now,
    To him all power is giv'n;
   To him in one communion bow
    All saints in earth and heaven.

5. While we, his soldiers, praise our King,
    His mercy we implore,
   Within his palace bright to bring
    And keep us evermore.

6. All glory to the Father be,
    All glory to the Son,
   All glory, Holy Ghost, to thee,
    While endless ages run. Alleluya!   Amen.

Translation by R. CAMPBELL (1814–1868)
and the compilers of *Hymns A & M*

Also available in *Hymns for Choirs* arr. David Willcocks

★CHOIR

6. All glo - ry to the Fa - ther be, All glo - ry to the Son,

ORGAN

Ped.

All glo - ry, Ho - ly Ghost, to thee, While end - less a - ges run.

Al - le - lu - ya! A - men.

*As an alternative to this choir part, the soprano part only may be sung as a descant.

App. 1. O little town of Bethlehem

Words by
PHILLIPS BROOKS
(1835–93)

H. WALFORD DAVIES
(1869–1941)

p 1. O lit - tle town of Beth - le-hem, How still we see thee lie!
mf 2. For Christ is born of Ma - ry; And, ga - ther'd all a - bove,
p 3. How si - lent-ly, how si - lent-ly, The won-drous gift is giv'n!
mp 4. O ho - ly Child of Beth - le-hem, Des - cend to us, we pray;

A - bove thy deep and dream-less sleep The si - lent stars go by.
While mor - tals sleep, the an - gels keep Their watch of wond-'ring love.
So God im - parts to hu - man hearts The bless-ings of his heav'n.
Cast out our sin, and en - ter in, Be born in us to - day.

mf Yet in thy dark streets shi - neth The ev - er - last - ing light;
f O morn - ing stars, to - geth - er Pro - claim the ho - ly birth,
cresc. No ear may hear his com - ing; But in this world of sin,
cresc. We hear the Christ-mas an - gels The great glad ti - dings tell:

The hopes and fears of all the years Are met in thee to - night.
And prais - es sing to God the King, And peace to men on earth!
mp Where meek souls will re - ceive him, still The dear Christ en - ters in.
O come to us, a - bide with us, Our Lord Em-man - u - el.

For the original extended version of this carol, see *Carols for Choirs 3*.

A FESTIVAL OF NINE LESSONS AND CAROLS

[The hymn Once in royal David's city *may be sung by the choir in procession, the congregation joining in the later verses.]*

¶ *The congregation, standing, shall be bidden to prayer in these words:*

Beloved in Christ, be it this Christmas Eve [*or* at this Christmas-tide] our care and delight to prepare ourselves to hear again the message of the Angels, and in heart and mind to go even unto Bethlehem and see this thing which is come to pass, and the Babe lying in a manger.

Therefore let us hear again from Holy Scripture the tale of the loving purposes of GOD from the first days of our sin unto the glorious Redemption brought us by this Holy Child: and let us make this (Chapel, dedicated to His pure and lowly Mother), glad with our carols of praise.

But first, because this of all things would rejoice His heart, let us pray to Him for the needs of the whole world, and all His people; for peace upon the earth He came to save; for love and unity within the one Church He did build; for brotherhood and goodwill amongst all men, (and especially within the dominions of our sovereign lady Queen Elizabeth, within this University and Town of Cambridge, and the two royal and religious Foundations of King Henry VI here and at Eton).

And particularly at this time let us remember before Him the poor, the cold, the hungry, the oppressed; the sick and them that mourn; the lonely and the unloved; the aged and the little children; all those who know not the Lord Jesus, or who love Him not, or who by sin have grieved His heart of love.

Lastly let us remember before Him them who rejoice with us, but upon another shore and in a greater light, that multitude which no man can number, whose hope was in the Word made flesh, and with whom, in this Lord Jesus, we for evermore are one.

These prayers and praises let us humbly offer up to the Throne of Heaven, in the words which Christ himself hath taught us:

Our Father, which [who] art in heaven, Hallowed be thy Name. Thy kingdom come. Thy will be done, in [on] earth as it is in heaven. Give us this day our daily bread. And forgive us our trespasses, As we forgive them that [those who] trespass against us. And lead us not into temptation; But deliver us from evil: For thine is the kingdom, the power, and the glory, For ever and ever. Amen.

The Almighty God bless us with His grace: Christ give us the joys of everlasting life: and unto the fellowship of the citizens above may the King of Angels bring us all. *Amen.*

¶ *Then shall the congregation sit.*

The readers of the lessons should be appointed after a definite order; in a cathedral, for instance, from chorister to bishop.
Each reader should announce the lesson by the descriptive sentence attached to it.
At the end of the lesson, the reader should pause and say: Thanks be to God.

FIRST LESSON   God tells sinful Adam that he has lost the life of Paradise and that his seed will bruise the serpent's head.   GENESIS 3: 8–15, 17–19

SECOND LESSON   God promises to faithful Abraham that in his seed shall all the nations of the earth be blessed.   GENESIS 22: 15–18

THIRD LESSON   The prophet foretells the coming of the Saviour.   ISAIAH 9: 2, 6–7

FOURTH LESSON   The peace that Christ will bring is foreshown.
ISAIAH 11: 1–4 (to 'meek of the earth'), 6–9

FIFTH LESSON   The angel Gabriel salutes the Blessed Virgin Mary.

ST LUKE 1: 26–35, 38

SIXTH LESSON   St Luke tells of the birth of Jesus.   ST LUKE 2: 1, 3–7

SEVENTH LESSON   The shepherds go to the manger.   ST LUKE 2: 8–16

EIGHTH LESSON   The wise men are led by the star to Jesus.   ST MATTHEW 2: 1–11

¶ *The congregation shall stand for the ninth lesson.*

NINTH LESSON   St John unfolds the great mystery of the Incarnation.

ST JOHN 1: 1–14

[*The hymn* O come, all ye faithful *is customarily sung here.*]

Minister: The Lord be with you.
People: And with thy spirit.

¶ *Then all shall kneel.*

Minister: Let us pray.

THE COLLECT FOR CHRISTMAS EVE*

O God, who makest us glad with the yearly remembrance of the birth of thy only Son, Jesus Christ: Grant that as we joyfully receive him for our redeemer, so we may with sure confidence behold him, when he shall come to be our judge; who liveth and reigneth with thee and the Holy Spirit, one God, world without end. *Amen.*

or THE COLLECT FOR CHRISTMAS DAY

Almighty God, who hast given us thy only-begotten Son to take our nature upon him, and as at this time to be born of a pure Virgin: Grant that we being regenerate, and made thy children by adoption and grace, may daily be renewed by thy Holy Spirit; through the same our Lord Jesus Christ, who liveth and reigneth with thee and the same Spirit, ever one God, world without end. *Amen.*

THE BLESSING

May he who by his Incarnation gathered into one things earthly and heavenly, fill you with the sweetness of inward peace and goodwill; and the blessing of God Almighty, the Father, the Son, and the Holy Ghost, be upon you and remain with you always. *Amen.*

*from the 1928 *Book of Common Prayer*

Note: In 1880 E. W. Benson, then Bishop of Truro, drew up a Festival of Nine Lessons and Carols, based on ancient sources, for use on Christmas Eve in the wooden shed which served as his cathedral. In 1918 this was adapted for use in the chapel of King's College, Cambridge by its Dean, Eric Milner-White, who also wrote the Bidding Prayer. This prayer is given here in its original version (with the sovereign's name changed). An altered version is given in *Carols for Choirs 1*, as are the complete texts of the Nine Lessons (including alternative fourth, fifth, and sixth lessons). The Blessing after the Lord's Prayer, added by Milner-White, was first included in its present form in 1930. The Nine Lessons given are those which have been customarily used in recent years at King's College.

INDEX OF CAROL ORCHESTRATIONS FOR HIRE (RENTAL)

In order to avoid delays at Christmas please place your hire order for carol orchestrations as early as possible. Please note WRITTEN, FAXED, or E-MAILED orders only will be accepted. Priority for orders will be established by the date received, not by the date of performance. Please quote the Hire Index number when ordering material.

Orchestrations are shown numerically to correspond with the traditional layout of an orchestral score, thus 2.2.2.2 - 4.3.3.1 - timp.hp - str indicates an orchestra comprising double woodwind, 4 horns, 3 trumpets, 3 trombones, tuba, timpani, harp and strings. Less commonly used instruments are shown by appropriate abbreviations within the numerical framework. (*) indicates that the item may be performed by strings only.

CAROL	SCORING	HIRE INDEX NO.
Adam lay ybounden	Strings	1
Angelus ad virginem	4tpt. 3tbn. tuba. chimes, bells, glock	141
As with gladness men of old	Strings	5
As with gladness men of old	Brass à 5	6
Away in a manger	Strings	9
babe is born, A	2.2.2.2 - 4.3.3.1 - timp.perc.pno. or cel. - str.	139
Birthday carol	Brass à 8 with percussion	11
Birthday carol	2.2.2.2 - 4.2.3.1 - perc. - str.	196
cherry tree carol, The	Strings	13
Child in a manger	2.2.2.1 - 0.0.0.0 - hp. [optional] - str.	150
child is born in Bethlehem, A	Strings	15
child is born in Bethlehem, A	Brass à 5	16
Christmas night	Strings	184
Ding dong! merrily on high	2.2.2.1 (or 2) - 2.0.0.0 perc. - str.	23
first Nowell, The	2.2.2.2 - 2.2.0.0 - timp. - str. (*)	26
first Nowell, The	Brass à 6 [see Five Carols from 'Carols for Choirs']	
Five Carols from 'Carols for Choirs'	3tpt. 3tbn. or 2tpt. 2hn. 2tbn. [each arr. with tba. timp. ad lib.]	27
God rest you merry, gentlemen	2.2.2.2 - 2.2.0.0 - pno. or org. - str. (*)	32
Good King Wenceslas	2.2.2.2 - 2.0.0.0 - str. (*)	253
Good King Wenceslas	Brass à 5	251
Good King Wenceslas	Brass à 6	252
great and mighty wonder, A	Strings with optional pno. or org.	37
Hark! the herald-angels sing	2.2.2.2 - 2.2.0.0 - [or 2.3.3.1] - timp.perc - str. (*)	38
Here we come a-wassailing	2.2.0.1 - 2.0.0.0 - perc.hp. - str.	41
Here we come a-wassailing	Brass à 8 with percussion and organ	128
I saw a fair mayden (Myn lyking)	Refer to William'Elkin Music Services (UK) Refer to G. Schirmer, Chester NY (USA)	
I saw three ships	2.2.2.2 - 2.0.0.0 - timp.perc.hp. - str.	133
I saw three ships	Brass à 8 with percussion and optional harp	152
Il est né le divin enfant	Strings and percussion	159
In the bleak mid-winter	2.2.2.2 - 2.0.0.0 - harp, strings	207
It came upon the midnight clear	2.2.2.1 (or 2) - 2.3.3.1 [or 2.2.0.0] - timp. - str. (*)	50
Jesus child	2fl. perc. bass. pno. or org.	53
Jesus child	2.2.2.1 - 2.0.0.0 - perc.hp. - str.	134
Jesus child	Brass à 8 with percussion and organ	136
Jingle, bells	2.2.2.2 - 4.3.3.1.timp.perc.org. - str.	187
Jingle, bells	Brass à 5	198
Jingle, bells	Brass à 8, percussion, organ	188

CAROL	SCORING	HIRE INDEX NO.
Joy to the world	2 tpt. timp. strings	186
Lo! he comes with clouds descending	2.2.2.2 - 4.4.3.1 - timp.perc. - str. (*)	181
Lo! he comes with clouds descending	Brass à 5	182
Lo! he comes with clouds descending	Brass à 8	183
Lute-book lullaby	Strings	57
maiden most gentle, A	Fl. ob. bn. str.	192
Mary's lullaby	Fl. ob. hp. str.	160
Nativity carol	Strings	59
O come, all ye faithful	2.2.2.2 - 2.3.3.1 [or 2.2.0.0] - timp.perc. - str. (*)	62
O come, all ye faithful	Brass à 6 [see Five Carols from 'Carols for Choirs']	
O come, o come, Emmanuel	2.2.2.2 - 2.3.3.1 [or 2.2.0.0] - timp. - str. (*)	65
O come, o come, Emmanuel	Brass à 8	67
Of the Father's heart begotten	2.2.2.2 - 2.3.3.1 [or 2.2.0.0] - timp. - str. (*)	69
O little town of Bethlehem (VW)	2.2.2.2 - 2.2.0.0 - str. (*)	71
O little town of Bethlehem (VW)	Brass à 5	72
O little town of Bethlehem (VW)	Brass à 6 [see Five Carols from 'Carols for Choirs']	
O little town of Bethlehem (Walford Davies)	2.2.2.2 - 2.2.2.1 - timp. strings	208
Once in royal David's city	2.2.2.2 - 2.2.3.1 [or 2.2.0.0] - timp. - str. (*)	76
Once in royal David's city	Brass à 8 with timpani	130
Personent hodie	Refer to William Elkin Music Services	
Quelle est cette odeur	Strings	79
Sans Day carol	2.2.0.1 - 2.0.0.0 - str.	87
See amid the winter's snow	2.2.2.2 - 2.2.0.0. - timp. - str.	88
See amid the winter's snow	Brass à 5	89
See amid the winter's snow	Brass à 6 [see Five Carols from 'Carols for Choirs']	
shepherds' farewell, The	2 ob. 2cl. str.	91
Shepherd's pipe carol	Fl. / picc. ob. bn. 2hn. hp. [optional] str.	93
Sir Christèmas	2.2.2.2 - 2.3.3.1 - timp.perc.org. or pno. - str. [optional: both hns. 3rd tpt. tuba perc. org. or pno.]; or Strings and organ or piano	100
Sir Christèmas	Brass [0.3.3.0 or 2.2.3.0] - timp.perc. [optional].org.	101
Star carol	2.2.2.2 - 2.0.0.0 - 2 perc.hp. - str.	103
Star carol	Brass à 8 with percussion	137
Still, still, still	Hp. and str.	191
Sussex carol	2picc. 2ob. 2cl. org. or pno. str. (*)	104
This Christmas night	Refer to Josef Weinberger Ltd (UK) Refer to Boosey & Hawkes Inc NYC (USA)	
twelve days of Christmas, The	1.2.0.1 - 2.0.0.0 - perc.hp. - str.	107
twelve days of Christmas, The	Brass à 8 with percussion and optional organ	108
Unto us is born a Son	2.2.2.2 - 2.2.0.0 - timp. - str. (*)	110
Unto us is born a Son	Brass à 6 [see Five Carols from 'Carols for Choirs']	
We wish you a merry Christmas	2.2.2.2 - 4.2.3.1 - timp.hp. - str.	117
We wish you a merry Christmas	Strings	115
We wish you a merry Christmas	Brass à 5 or à 6 with percussion	116
While shepherds watched	2.2.2.1 [or 2] - 2.2.0.0 [or 2.3.3.1] - timp. - str.	121
Ye choirs of new Jerusalem	Brass à 8	Hymns for Choirs